"The study was well thought out and organized in a way that made it easy to understand. I liked the way it was divided up and brought scriptures and their meanings together. It brought me greater appreciation of the awesomeness of God."

—Paula Cannon,
Elementary Education Teacher, Rowlett, Texas

"As this study guided me through the beautiful promises of Psalm 119, I fell even more in love with the character of God. His words are life-giving, life-changing, and life-directing. The cross-references to other scripture reinforced how rich and true God's word is. I know I will refer back to Blessings Beyond the Page for years to come."

—Amanda Byrd,
Nurse Practitioner and Business Owner, Rockwall, Texas

"I really enjoyed the thought put into this Bible study. You could tell that Chantal created it with others in mind. It was spacious, thought provoking, and a safe place to meet with God while digging into one of the most intense Psalms. I look forward to the next study I attend with Chantal!"

—Caroline Tamez,
Pastoral Care Coordinator for women with unexpected pregnancies, Watermark Church, Dallas, Texas

"The Lord has trails for me to take on my path here and home to Him. Psalm 119 helps me with the right turn on those trails. One of them led me to Chantal Johnson, who has opened her home to allow her Bible studies to guide me in the right turns. This study in Psalm 119 recharges me when things get tough. It's my safe place to regain refuge when life has speed bumps. I treasure and love the word of God. With this Bible study, it is a lamp unto our feet and the light to the right turns to our path home."

—Denice (Niecy) Drum,
Transportation, Garland Independent School District,
Garland, Texas

BLESSINGS BEYOND THE PAGE

A Study of PSALM 119

CHANTAL JOHNSON

LUCIDBOOKS

Blessings Beyond the Page: A Study of Psalm 119

Published by Lucid Books in Houston, TX
www.LucidBooks.com

ISBN: 978-1-63296-701-5

eISBN: 978-1-63296-642-1

Special Sales: Most Lucid Books titles are available in special quantity discounts. Custom imprinting or excerpting can also be done to fit special needs. Contact Lucid Books at Info@LucidBooks.com

To my daddy who has taught me to walk with the Lord even when the way is hard and the steps are steep. Daddy taught me to hold Jesus' hand when I lose my footing and to grab hold of His words and bring them close so that when the way seems unnavigable, I can hear the Lord say to me, "Here is the way, walk in it."

When Daddy bought a new Bible for me in 1984, it was a beautiful leather-bound edition; the paper was a crisp white with Jesus' words in red. Fast-forward almost 40 years, the pages have handwritten reminders of meaning and insight, verses are highlighted, many pages are dog-eared, the leather cover is worn, and the spine is separated in places. However, the letters in red are perfectly intact. These are the precious words that give life and meaning.

Daddy wrote an inscription in my Bible that I would like to pass on to you:

—Stay close to these words all the days of your life.

Love, Daddy

TABLE OF CONTENTS

INTRODUCTION

Making the most of our time with God

CREATING PLANS AND PROJECTS

Come join me for a study of Psalm 119 where the love of God, His word, and the love of all things creative combine for a time of Bible study, inspiration, and fun while we share and create beautiful reminders of His love for us.

This is how my invitation to acquaintances, friends, and family begins. As one who loves to study God's word, I take pleasure in offering my home as a place to gather and learn together with fellow believers. As an artist, I realize that we need creative, beautiful, simple reminders to connect with God's word in a new, lasting way. Too often, when we finish a Bible study, we close our books or journals and put them on the shelf. And over time, some of the precepts, promises, and praises get buried a little further in our memory.

In the Old Testament, we read:

> *These commandments that I give you today are to be on your hearts. Impress them on your children. Talk about them when you sit at home and when you walk along the road, when you lie down and when you get up. Tie them as symbols on your hands and bind them on your foreheads. Write them on the doorframes of your houses and on your gates.*
>
> —Deuteronomy 6:6–9

In other words, we are to let the words of God be in every area of our lives not just on our bookshelves; we are to let them move beyond the page and into our hearts and homes, onto our walls, and even into our wardrobe. So how can we create beautiful reminders as we study Psalm 119 or any Scripture? What can we do to bring His word into our conversations, onto our commutes, and around our coffee tables? In this Introduction, I offer a few ideas and instructions—a creative plan along with a few creative project suggestions—to demonstrate how you can use this study to bring the love of God and His word into your home or wherever you gather to learn more of Him.

This study of Psalm 119 is designed as a 5-week study consisting of two main parts:

- Part 1, "Thy Word in my Heart" focuses on five ways we approach God's Word (i.e., obey, seek, study, meditate, and rejoice) with the key verse being Psalm 119:11.
- Part 2, "Daily in His Word," focuses on 20 blessings we receive as we read God's word using key verses from Psalm 119.

Each part features a Daily Precept (key verse) and a Daily Ponder (verse to meditate) with space for you to write, reflect, praise, and pray.

Both parts are ideal for use either as individual or group study. In this book, Part 1 is presented as Week 1 of a 5-week study; it is listed as Days 1–5. Part 2 is presented as Days 1–20 of the remaining 4 weeks of the study.

However, please note that the material is flexible; you have various options to customize it to fit your needs. For instance, Part 1 may stand alone and be used for a seminar weekend or retreat, Part 2 goes deeper into Psalm 119 and may be used as a 4-week individual study. The two parts blend together and may be presented as a 5-week small group or individual study.

CREATIVE PLANS

Sometimes, when we prepare to study God's word, we grab the Bible, open it to a verse, read the Scripture passage and then think—now what? Or we try to squeeze our study in between morning coffee and carpool. I would like to suggest a few creative plans for studying and sharing *Blessings Beyond the Page* so that you will be blessed by your efforts.

CREATIVE STUDY FOR INDIVIDUALS

- Gather all your materials such as your Bible, *Blessing Beyond the Page*, highlighter, pen, commentary (if desired, but not needed) and place them all in a basket or a bag, so that all your materials are ready when you are.
- Find a place in your home or wherever you choose to study that is beautiful to you. Pleasant surroundings can be a catalyst to help you stay focused and linger over His word.

- Read Scripture verses in more than one translation; different Bible versions can prompt new thoughts—especially with familiar Scripture passage. A different version can spark an image or a nuance to a verse that you may have read over and over again.
- Find a daily rhythm and establish a time that works in your everyday routine.
- For each of the precept or ponder verses, write the verse and as much as you can about your observations. When we read and write the words of Scripture, our minds grab hold of them and will bring them to our thoughts and words in our day, creating greater impact in our lives.

CREATIVE STUDY WITH GROUPS

If you are leading or facilitating a small group or gathering, consider using a few of these ideas to create an atmosphere that is welcoming to all and that serves as a reminder of His love and His word.

- Name tags! Print, make, or write name tags; this is an easy way to ensure that each member of the group is known. Having names tags means that newcomers won't feel pressure to memorize everyone's name. Provide name tags each week!
- If you are leading a gathering in a home, serve refreshments and/or invite others to participate in bringing refreshments. Be sure to allow time for people to get to know one another. This can be a shared responsibility, but never underestimate the importance of hospitality—it creates an inviting atmosphere for everyone.

- Create a bookmark for each member or have each member create their own, to be used throughout the study. The bookmark can be as simple as cardstock with a printed verse—whatever your creativity, time, and resources permit. I have used a variety of bookmarks from beaded bookmarks to laminated notepaper to large paperclips with tassels. Choose symbols such as hearts to carry out the theme of the study.
- Print verse card downloads to be given to each small group member each week.
- When I prepare for the studies that I teach, I prepare a scripture bag that includes the study guide, highlighter, pen, Week 1 verse cards, and a bookmark for each member of the group.
- For each following week, I prepare the verse cards for that week and add a small item, which serves as a reminder of one of the verses. For example, I might include pineapple candy (i.e., hospitality), a small vial of bubbles (i.e., His word bubbles over), a flower seed packet (i.e., the word of God is planted . . .), or a spur charm (i.e., let us spur one another on to good works), and so on. This is a way to add reminders of God in the daily. Keep tokens simple and only do what you can do; remember that the intention of the heart is to help share the goodness of God's word in tangible ways.
- Feel free to lead the group in doing art projects that come from the verses themselves—whatever helps participants see what is spoken of or taught in the verses. For example, when I taught on the armor of God, we made belt bracelet cuffs from vintage belts and snaps using a snap setter.

SUGGESTED TIMELINE FOR GROUP STUDY

The facilitator/group leader has the following responsibilities.

Week 1 – Introduction:

- Distribute *Blessings Beyond the Page* (include a scripture bag, if possible).
- Share refreshments or a meal and allow time for the group to get to know one another.
- Give an overview of the study and the format of each day along with the overall schedule for your study.
- Remind everyone that what is shared in the group stays in the group and remind them to only share what you are comfortable with.
- Encourage participation.
- If you choose to use creative reminders, create a bookmark or verse holder.

Weeks 2 – 6:

- Distribute verse cards (and reminders, if possible).
- Share and review the previous week's study activities.
- Share refreshments or a meal and allow time for the group to get to know one another.
- If you choose to use creative reminders, add art projects and beautiful reminders.

No matter what is created, given, or shared in this study, the most important matter is the Creator and what He has given to us and shared with us—His love, His grace, His kindness, His ever-present help, His faithful word, His Son, and His Spirit. Remember, that whatever we do, we do it all for Him, and when we share His amazing word with others, He brings blessings beyond the page and into our heart, our home, our group, our community, and our world.

Creating Places of Precepts and Praise

Surround Your Surroundings with God's Word

One day when my son was in college, he took photographs inside our home and although he had seen it all before, when he looked at the pictures, he commented, "Wow, you have a lot of words, Mom." And to that, I replied, "Yes, I do." Words on the wall, words above the fireplace, even words on our napkins and my jewelry. But these are not just ordinary words; they are God's words that offer hope, joy, love, and direction—words that invite us to praise. Here are a few ideas of how to bring His word into your home and heart.

- Mornings can begin with a message on a mug, cup, or even a napkin.
- Evenings can end with a thoughtful moment or prayer, reflecting on the day.
- Set time every day to read and reflect on His word.
- Verse cards on mirrors, dashboard, refrigerator, and/or displayed throughout your home.
- His word on notepads or plaques, in picture frames, or on pillows and dish towels—wherever it will be visible as you go about your day.
- Daily Scripture journals, praise and gratitude journals, or remembering journals.
- Handwritten Scriptures or Bible studies that focus on an area of concern or growth.
- Heart verses on phones, prayers recorded in notes (on phone).
- Music that uplifts and brings praise.
- Books and articles that point to God, His word, His values, etc.

- Wardrobe reminders through jewelry and clothes.
- Seeing His beauty in all things lovely, pure, excellent, true, and worthy.
- Speaking life and blessings to others and yourself.
- Bringing beauty in through nature as this points to the natural beauty of God.

Ponder these application questions:

- What are some ways you bring His word into your surroundings?
- What are some new ways you would like to bring His word in your surroundings?

PSALM 119

Psalms 119 is the longest chapter in the Bible, consisting of 176 verses. And although we do not know who wrote this psalm, we do know that the psalmist loves the Author of Life and that he finds his greatest treasure in the Word of God. The psalmist searches the Scriptures to know the heart of God and the hope of His love for us.

Psalm 119 is an acrostic poem made up of 22 stanzas written in the order of the Hebrew alphabet; each stanza begins with a letter, and then the first line of each verse in that stanza begins with the same letter. The time and attention that the psalmist gave to the words inspired by the Holy Spirit convey the depth of his love for our God who is not only in the big picture, but in the very details of our lives. For your convenience, this book includes the New International Version (NIV) of Psalm 119 as well as the Hebrew text. Take a look for just a moment at the Hebrew version and notice the letters that begin each line of each stanza.

Scripture tells us that He knows when a sparrow falls, and He knows the number of hairs on our head. He is worthy, oh so worthy, of the time and attention we will devote to studying this most precious treasure, His word. May we read the words of Psalm 119 and other texts with an undivided heart and a loyal love.

PART 1:

THY WORD IN MY HEART – A STUDY OF PSALM 119

I have hidden thy word in my heart that I might not sin against you.

—Psalm 119:11

There are so many catchphrases, buzz words, and cliches that mean well and look cute on a mug or t-shirt but come short in delivery. Some may even have hidden meanings or prompt more questions than answers on second thought. For example:

- "You are enough." Enough what? Like, I have had enough or enough said?
- "Follow your own arrow." To where? Aim at what? What is my arrow?
- "Let nature be your teacher." Which part—the tornadoes and hurricanes? Rolling hills or ant hills?
- "Be a pineapple, stand tall and wear a crown." I didn't know we could be fruit or better yet, tall.

- "Never go in search of love, instead go in search of life and life will find you the love you seek." How do we even address this one? Where is life exactly? And how do I search for life? Does life know love?

As we search for words to live by—words to learn from and shape our thinking and ultimately, to give our life meaning—where do we start? Psalm 119 comprises holy, inspired phrases that give us a direction and show us the path on which to walk. This psalm is filled with powerful words that we can hide, treasure, and store in our hearts—words that will teach us who we are and what we are to become.

As we study this psalm, we will see that love is the motivation for following God's word. And by seeking God, studying His word, and meditating on His love and His beautiful character, we can live a life of praise. We will be filled with His presence as we hide His Word in our hearts.

Let's turn the page and give Him the pen, inviting the author of life and love to write on our hearts the words we need to live life abundantly.

> May your heart overflow with praise as your love grows deeper for the Lord.
>
> —Chantal

> *This has been my practice: I obey your precepts.*
>
> —Psalm 119:56

> *Your word is a lamp for my feet, a light on my path.*
>
> —Psalm 119:105

> *The unfolding of your word gives light: it gives understanding to the simple.*
>
> —Psalm 119:130

Our responsibility and our response to His word in our hearts:

Walk
Keep
Follow
Consider
Obey
Hide, treasure, store
Recount
Teach
Meditate
Delight
Long for

Put my hope in
Trust
Love
Wholeheartedly follow
Ponder
Set on
Regard for
Stand in awe
Rejoice
Chosen

OVERVIEW

I have heard it said that God has given us the best book (His word), the best place (our hearts), and the best purpose (to live for Him). When we take His word and hide it in our hearts (Psalm 119:11), we have a path and a purpose. This psalm teaches us to seek God and His direction in all things through His word with all our heart (the inner person, soul, and mind). Therefore, the more we are in His word, the more we see His love and His blessings. As you work through this study, you will find key words, key verses, and key themes that point to the reason why we follow Him. We follow because we love Him, and we seek to learn because of His great love for us.

Key Words in Psalm 119: Learn, seek, teach, obey, meditate, praise, follow, walk, run, path, unfailing love, trust, sustain, direct, understanding, word, commands, law, decrees, statutes, precepts, promise, hope in, life.

Key Verses: 11, 56, 68, 89, 105, 169–173 (Note that every verse in Psalm 119 except verse 5 points to or refers to God's word.)

Key Themes:

- God's love is the force and the foundation of His word.
- Choose to follow and obey.

- Know, remember, recount, hold on to His word.
- Desire to learn, to understand.
- Live a life for and with God.
- Praise for God's word.
- Holding on to His promise(s).
- God is good; what he does is good.
- Unfailing love sustains us.
- In times of selfishness, turn my heart to His word.
- In times of adversity or trouble, turn and meditate on His word.
- In times of distraction, turn my eyes to His word.

Key Scriptures:

To treasure or store God's word in our hearts, we have to be in His word. The following Scriptures can be the beginning or an addition to studying His word. From Jesus' words in Matthew, to the words of Moses and the Ten Commandments, to Solomon's wise words, to encouraging words from Paul and Peter, these verses can speak into our hearts the very nature of God and into our lives the way He would have us go:

Matthew 5–7
Exodus 20 (the Ten Commandments)
Proverbs: Read one chapter each day (31 chapters)
1 Thessalonians 5:16–18
Colossians 3–4, James, 1 Peter

Key Definitions:

The following terms are used throughout Psalm 119. You may find it helpful to refer to this list as you work through the study and become familiar with what these terms mean in the context of this psalm:

- *Commands:* Broad principle of how we are to obey and show love to God; straight authority (His power).
- *Promise:* General word for God's law.
- *Precepts:* A rule or direction (behavior); "life lesson." The Lord cares about the details in our lives; He is not too busy or burdened.
- *Statutes:* To inscribe or cut in; to "set in stone"; boundaries for life
- *Decrees:* Unchangeable, holy, wise, eternal purpose (statement of fact)
- *Word:* Speaks to all people; a guide for living; embracing God's truth; grace
- *Ways:* The will of God; leads to life; reflection of God's good character
- *Law:* Single command or the whole body of Scripture; revelation
- *Testimonies*: The law testifies to the truth of God's faithful word. We are the testimony of His word.

WEEK 1: DAILY IN HIS WORD

Each day's study includes time for the following focus areas: precept, ponder, practice, praise, progress, and prayer.

Daily Precept: **His truth, His word.**
From the Scripture selected, write down the precept verse(s) and your observations.

Daily Ponder: **His nature or character.**
In this precept verse, what is being revealed about God and His nature/character?
Record your observations, asking how you can meditate, ponder, or consider this aspect of God's nature.

Daily Practice: **His direction.**
How do/will you follow in your daily life?
List practical ways or applications.

Daily Praise: **Your response to His word.**
Why is this precept praiseworthy?
Write expressions of your gratitude, hope, praise, or prayer. You can even write Scripture for your response.

Daily Progress: **A summary of what His word (i.e., the Precept verse) teaches is provided by the author.** Comment on where He is leading you each day.

Daily Prayer: **A moment of prayer.** You may use the prayer in the daily prayer section or write your own.

WEEK 1 DAILY PLAN

Day 1: **Obedience**—to follow, to keep His word.

Day 2: **Seek**—to search out the important things of God and His word.

Day 3: **Study**—to learn, to be teachable to grow in grace, understanding, faith, and love.

Day 4: **Meditate**—to ponder, consider; filling our minds with God and His goodness; to pause, think on, and reflect.

Day 5: **Rejoice**—to recite or recount; to praise as we follow, learn, and remember.

Dear Heavenly Father,

As we begin this study, we see that you have poured not only your love but your words into our hearts and lives. May we choose to follow you all the days of our lives. And in our days, may we seek you through your Spirit-filled words and, most of all, through the Word of life, Jesus. May we delight in studying, meditating, knowing, and rejoicing in your word. Increase our understanding, not for selfish gain but for saving and sustaining grace. Increase our devotion to the One who devoted His life (and death) for us. May we share your life-giving words in ways that touch the hearts of those who do not know you. May we hide and treasure your word as we live for and with you. As we turn each page and read each verse, open our eyes and fill our hearts with the sweetest words, rich in grace, mercy, and love.

In Jesus' name. Amen.

GETTING STARTED

My Heart

When we want to grow in any area of our life, we must first begin with desire, followed by setting a direction and applying devotion. When we plant seeds in rich soil or flowers in a clay pot, the desire is fulfilled and the direction is known, but then devotion happens daily. Daily routines of watering, weeding, nurturing, and gathering are some of the ways we take care of our gardens. Daily routines can also be daily rhythms that set our hearts toward growth in our faith, our marriage, our relationships, and our love.

Take a moment to set a direction for this study and then identify or create a daily rhythm or two that will enrich the soil of your heart.

My Goals

Daily Direction/Daily Rhythm

1.

2.

3.

DAY 1

How can a young person stay on the path of purity? By living according to your word.

—Psalm 119:9

Don't just listen to the Word of Truth and not respond to it, for that is the essence of self-deception. So always let his Word become like poetry written and fulfilled by your life!

—James 1:22 TPT

In fact, this is love for God: to keep his commands. And his commands are not burdensome.

—1 John 5:3

If you keep my commands, you will remain in my love, just as I have kept my Father's commands and remain in his love.

—John 15:10

Give me understanding [a teachable heart and the ability to learn], that I may keep Your law; And observe it with all my heart.

—Psalm 119:34 AMP

DAY 1 – TO OBEY, TO FOLLOW, TO KEEP

Psalm 119:9, John 15:10, James 1:22–25, 1 John 5:3

Daily Precept: Psalm 119:9

Daily Ponder: Psalm 119:34

DAY 1 - TO OBEY, TO FOLLOW, TO KEEP

Daily Practice:

Daily Praise:

DAY 1 – TO OBEY, TO FOLLOW, TO KEEP

Daily Progress:

We all live by something or someone. It could be that we live by the world's standards, which are ever-shifting, ever-changing, or we may live by our own standards—our heart or feelings, our likes or dislikes, which are also ever-shifting and ever-changing. We must remember that the heart (without Jesus) is deceitful above all things, and we are naturally selfish. Believers live by God's standard—His word that He has provided. His word is changeless, timeless, and fresh every time we open the pages of Scripture.

When we have a teachable heart and a desire to learn, His word is not beyond our ability to understand. It's OK to not know or understand everything in Scripture; we'll spend our lifetime learning. There is, however, enough that we can understand to begin living the Christian life. For instance, we know what we are to be thankful, love one another, offer hospitality, be generous, and share the good news of Jesus.

We can ask Him for a desire to know and to read His word. We can ask for a love of His word to be placed in our hearts so that we can obey His word from a place of love and not just duty or drudgery.

Daily Prayer:

> Father, direct my heart to long to learn more of who Jesus is. May the pages of Scripture, your word, be the best part of my story!
>
> In the name of Jesus, the author and perfector of our faith. Amen.

DAY 2

I seek you with all my heart;
do not let me stray from your commands.

—Psalm 119:10

You will seek me and find me when you seek me with all your heart.

—Jeremiah 29:13

But seek first his kingdom and his righteousness, and all these things will be given to you as well.

—Matthew 6:33

Ask and keep on asking and it will be given to you; seek and keep seeking and you will find; Knock and keep on knocking and the door will be opened to you.

—Matthew 7:7 AMP

Turn from evil and do good; seek peace and pursue it.

—Psalm 34:14

DAY 2 – TO SEEK, TO LOOK FOR

Psalm 119:10, Jeremiah 29:13, Matthew 6:33, Matthew 7:7

Daily Precept: Psalm 119:10

Daily Ponder: Psalm 34:14

DAY 2 – TO SEEK, TO LOOK FOR

Daily Practice:

Daily Praise:

DAY 2 – TO SEEK, TO LOOK FOR

Daily Progress:

When we seek Him through His word, we receive eyes to see, ears to hear, and hearts to understand. He gives us a heavenly perspective. In the word, the heart is the center of everything, the core of our being; this is not the world's view of the heart, which is fashioned after feelings. We are to set our hearts on His word, the foundation of our lives.

In this life, we are actively seeking someone or something. Whatever we seek, we seek with the intention of bringing the heart of God, the love of Jesus, and His word to the place we are in and to the people we are with. When we seek God in the daily, we will find ways to worship, to be content, to make time to know His word, and to do good by finding someone to help, something to give, and somewhere to serve.

What is trying to steal your joy and get your heart off-center? Find the chaos, disorder, and distractions and turn away; turn to Jesus. Seek Him and His commands, which are not burdensome. Speak life, love, and truth to your heart and into your circumstance.

Daily Prayer:

> Father, thank you, that you are not far away—neither sleeping nor hard of hearing. Thank you for pouring out your love in my heart, so that I can give your love to others. May I seek you first!
>
> In the name of Jesus, the One who is always near. Amen.

DAY 3

You are good, and what you do is good; teach me your decrees.

—Psalm 119:68

But the Advocate, the Holy Spirit, whom the Father will send in my name, will teach you all things and will remind you of everything I have said to you.

—John 14:26

For everything that was written in the past was written to teach us, so that through the endurance taught in the Scriptures and the encouragement they provide we might have hope.

—Romans 15:4

Command and teach these things. Don't let anyone look down on you because you are young, but set an example for the believers in speech, in conduct, in love, in faith and in purity. Until I come, devote yourself to the public reading of Scripture, to preaching and to teaching.

—1 Timothy 4:11–13

Show me your ways, Lord, *teach me your paths. Guide me in your truth and teach me, for you are God my Savior, my hope is in you all day long.*

—Psalm 25:4–5

DAY 3 – TO STUDY, TO LEARN, TO BE TEACHABLE

Psalm 119:68, John 14:26, Romans 15:4, 1 Timothy 4:11–13

Daily Precept: Psalm 119:68

Daily Ponder: Psalm 25:4–5

DAY 3 – TO STUDY, TO LEARN, TO BE TEACHABLE

Daily Practice:

Daily Praise:

Day 3 - To Study, to Learn, to Be Teachable

Daily Progress:

We need to know and believe that He is good and that His word is good. The word brings hope when we read and receive it from His heart of love—His heart of healing and His heart of forgiveness. We must be listening for His truth, looking for His ways, learning His path, and leaning on His saving grace.

We study to have hope, which does not disappoint. We pray, asking for a heart of a student, a lifelong learner. As we learn, we set an example for others and then we, in turn, can teach others.

If Jesus is most important in our lives, then our convictions, our choices, and our conversations need to align with His word. Our opinions are no longer important. And if this is a struggle for you, know that it is for me too. We must ask the Lord for his kindness and his patience as we surrender our ways and our thoughts to Him.

Daily Prayer:

> Thank you for your way, your path, your truth, and your words. You write your name on my heart, and you write my name on your hand. You give me wisdom and understanding. You are love, and what you do is lovely. Help me see that your words and ways bring a beautiful life and that your will for me is to the follow the greatest teacher, who is the way, the truth, and the life. Let me learn the way of love, Jesus.
>
> In the name of Jesus, the love and kindness of God. Amen.

DAY 4

I meditate [set my heart] on your precepts and consider your ways.

—Psalm 119:15

Lord, as we worship you in your temple, we recall over and over your kindness to us and your unending love.

—Psalm 48:9 TPT

I will consider all your works and meditate on all your mighty deeds.

—Psalm 77:12

Set your minds on things above, not on earthly things.

—Colossians 3:2

Reflect on what I am saying, for the Lord will give you insight into all this.

—2 Timothy 2:7

DAY 4 - TO MEDITATE, TO PONDER, TO CONSIDER, TO REFLECT

Psalm 119:15, Psalm 48:9, Psalm 77:12, Colossians 3:2

Daily Precept: Psalm 119:15

Daily Ponder: 2 Timothy 2:7

DAY 4 – TO MEDITATE, TO PONDER, TO CONSIDER, TO REFLECT

Daily Practice:

Daily Praise:

DAY 4 – TO MEDITATE, TO PONDER, TO CONSIDER, TO REFLECT

Daily Progress:

To meditate means to think on, to fill our minds with, or to consider; it is faith-forward thinking. When we meditate, we empty our minds of the worries of the world and fill them with the wonders and words of God. When we worship, our minds are centered on His kindness and His unending love.

God's thoughts always take me higher, and I begin to think with a heavenly mindset. I begin with Jesus on my mind. When we honor His word, we will respect His desire and direction for our lives. If we do not pause to consider, we will rush into decisions without the Lord.

With our minds set on things above, our intuition responds to the guiding of the Holy Spirit, and we will be grounded in His word. Another word for mediation is *linger.* Let us not linger in disobedience but linger with the One who abides in us and calls us to obey.

Daily Prayer:

> Jesus, help me to linger over your words and to lift them from the pages of Scripture and bring them to life as I set my heart upon you, the Word of life.
>
> In the name of Jesus, the One who invites us to stay. Amen.

DAY 5

I will praise you with an upright heart as I learn your righteous laws.

—Psalm 119:7

I speak continually of your laws as I recite out loud your counsel to me.

—Psalm 119:13 TPT

I will tell of the LORD*'s unfailing love. I will praise the* LORD *for all he has done. I will rejoice in his great goodness to Israel, which he has granted according to his mercy and love.*

—Isaiah 63:7 NLT

Then those who feared the LORD *talked with each other, and the* LORD *listened and heard. A scroll of remembrance was written in his presence concerning those who feared the* LORD *and honored his name.*

—Malachi 3:16

Therefore, encourage one another with these words.

—1 Thessalonians 4:18

Let praise cascade off my lips; after all, you've taught me the truth about life!

—Psalm 119:171 MSG

DAY 5 – TO REJOICE, TO RECITE, TO RECOUNT

Psalm 119:7, Psalm 119:13, Isaiah 63:7, Malachi 3:16, 1 Thessalonians 4:18

Daily Precept: Psalm 119:7, 13

Daily Ponder: Psalm 119:171

DAY 5 - TO REJOICE, TO RECITE, TO RECOUNT

Daily Practice:

Daily Praise:

DAY 5 - TO REJOICE, TO RECITE, TO RECOUNT

Daily Progress:

In typical conversations, we praise, rejoice, speak continually, and tell of God's wonderful works. We encourage and speak blessings over others. Our words will be remembered. May they offer hope, overflow with kindness, be seasoned with grace, be filled with thanksgiving, and even burst into song (if so, moved by the Spirit). And may our words and songs be Jesus—all day, every day!

We become a testimony to His word. When we speak, let our words be grace-filled, hope-saturated, and kindness-infused. We hold out the Word of Life. Let those who hear us hear truth, love, and salvation.

In Psalm 119:7, the words *"As I learn"* mean that learning is continual, daily, moment by moment; class is always in session. And as we learn more of God's word, there will be a change, a transformation. In our daily moments, praise flows, gratitude grows, and hope is planted.

In Malachi 3:16, we read of the scroll of remembrance. The Lord listened then, and He listens now, as a Father to his children, to hear whether what has been taught has been caught in our hearts and then released into our character and conversation.

Daily Prayer:

Thank you for not tiring of me as I learn your word. And when I need to re-learn, thank you for your patience, your grace, and your loving-kindness! Your goodness is overwhelming, especially when I get the lesson wrong, when I mess up, and when I speak unkind and harsh words. May I remember that my words reflect my heart. Lord, create in me a pure heart that I may have a renewed spirit within me—Your Spirit of love, grace, and truth. Breathe new words into my tired and tried heart. May I seek, obey, study, meditate, and praise you all the days of my life, for you have put "The Life" in all my days.

In the name of Jesus, the One who is The Life. Amen.

DAILY TREASURES

Here are more verses to treasure in your heart:

Obey

Psalm 119:2, 8, 17, 34, 57, 67, 100, 129, 166, 167
Deuteronomy 30:16
Joshua 1:9
Psalm 34:12–16
Philippians 2:6–12
Romans 2:13
2 John 1:6

Seek

Psalm 119:2, 58
Acts 17:27
1 Corinthians 10:24

Study

Psalm 119:12, 24, 26, 32–33, 64, 66, 68, 105, 120, 124, 135
Proverbs 1:5; 23:12
Luke 24:27

Meditate

Psalm 119:15, 23, 27, 48, 78, 97, 99, 148
Psalm 1:2; 27:14; 31:16; 104:34
Psalm 107:43; 111:2; 143:5
Luke 2:19

Praise

Psalm 119:7, 12–16, 35, 46, 62, 103, 108, 131, 145–147, 162, 164, 171–172, 175
Psalm 1:2
Proverbs 7:1; 16:21
Daniel 4:2
Matthew 9:3; Luke 6:45; 1 Peter 3:15

When you feel…	**Meditate on…**
Defeated	You have the victory that overcomes the world.
Alone	Never will He leave you, nor forsake you.
Unloved	He has loved you with an everlasting love.
Shaken	He will sustain you and never let you be shaken.
Scared, uncertain	Do not worry about tomorrow.
Hopeless	Hope in Jesus is our anchor.
Empty	He fills us with joy.
Hurt	He heals the brokenhearted.
Misunderstood	He formed my heart; He considers all I do.
Too far	Draw near to God, and He will draw near to you.
Too broken	He is close to the brokenhearted.
Guilt, shame	There is no condemnation for those who are in Jesus.
Betrayal	His unfailing love and kindness surrounds you.
Lonely	He sets the lonely in families.
Weary	He is our rest.
Lost	I am found, for He is my Savior.

Other Scripture Treasures:

1 John 5:4
1 Corinthians 15:57
Hebrews 13:5
Jeremiah 31:3
Psalm 55:25
Matthew 6:25–34
Hebrews 6:19
Romans 15:13
Psalm 147:3
1 Corinthians 1:2–4
Psalm 33:13–15
Romans 8:1
Psalm 85:7
1 Samuel 20:14
Lamentations 3:2
Psalm 68:6
Psalm 62:5
Luke 19:10

We run in the way of His commands; we walk in freedom because of His precepts; we speak of His statutes; we set our hearts on His decrees; we rise with hope in His word; we rest with His promises; we live to praise Him; and we stand in awe of the Word of Life, Jesus.

The more we read, the more we learn and the more we learn, the more we know. The more we know, the more we love Jesus. The more we love Jesus, the more we learn of Jesus, and so a lifelong learner is born. This introduction to Psalm 119 is just the beginning of the blessings we receive from His word. His word shares His heart and His hope, His desires and His direction, His gifts and His grace, and His Son and His salvation.

In Part 2, we will discover 20 of the many blessings to be found in Psalm 119—blessings that we receive daily in our every circumstance. As we continue to be lifelong learners, the Lord will bring blessings beyond the page!

Blessings as you daily dig deeper!!

PART 2:

DAILY 4-WEEK STUDY OF PSALMS 119

God, teach me lessons for living so I can stay the course.
—Psalm 119:33 MSG

We read many ads, posts, stories, and reels that may inspire us to buy, sell, cook, or create, but often they just stay on the page or the screen of our phone. We might bookmark or save them or open a web browser, but after all that, they are just words on a page. Books that we read may provide a lesson learned or even a love story that brings us to tears, but most stories don't withstand the test of time, and we are left with new lessons that require new words. Words we read and leave where we find them have little to no value in our daily living.

But Psalm 119 is different: It consists of His words—living, fresh words. If we obey them, seek them, study them, mediate and rejoice over them, He showers us with blessings beyond the page. Psalm 119 gives us at least 20 blessings that come from the words of the psalmist. These are blessings that withstand the test of time; provide answers for life's lessons; and make an eternal mark over our lives. From revealing the path of life to making provisions for our life, from giving comfort and care to providing hope and freedom, this psalm shows how God's Word—not just read but lived—is our guide, our protection, our refuge, and our foundation. And because God's word became flesh and dwelt among us, we see Jesus leave the pages of Scripture and walk with us—becoming the greatest blessing beyond the page.

Let's turn the page and see how God's word lives in us.

> May your life be the story of His words, His love, and His grace.
>
> —Chantal

DAILY IN HIS WORD

Each day's study includes time for the following focus areas: precept, ponder, praise, progress, and prayer.

Daily Precept: **His truth, His word.**
From the Scripture selected, write down the precept verse(s) and your observations.

Daily Ponder: **His nature or character.**
In this precept verse, what is being revealed about God and His nature/character?
Record your observations, asking how you can meditate, ponder, or consider this aspect of God's nature.

Daily Practice: **His direction.**
How do/will you follow in your daily life?
List practical ways or applications.

Daily Praise: **Your response to His Word.**
Why is this precept praiseworthy?
Write expressions of gratitude, hope, praise, or prayer. You can even write Scripture for your response.

Daily Progress: **A summary of what His word (i.e., the Precept verse) teaches is provided by the author.**
Comment on where He is leading you each day.

Daily Prayer: **A moment of prayer.**
You may use the prayer in the daily prayer section or write your own.

My Heart

When we want to grow in any area of our life, we must first begin with desire, followed by setting a direction and applying devotion. When we plant seeds in rich soil or flowers in a clay pot, the desire is fulfilled, and the direction is known, but then devotion happens daily. Daily routines of watering, weeding, nurturing, and gathering are some of the ways we take care of our gardens. Daily routines can also be daily rhythms that set our hearts toward growth in our faith, our marriage, our relationships, and our love.

Take a moment to set a direction for this study and then identify or create a daily rhythm or two that will enrich the soil of your heart.

My Goals

Daily Direction/Daily Rhythm

1.

2.

3.

Dear Heavenly Father,

As we begin this study, may our love for your word grow deeper, may we see our blessings abound in and through your word. And when we hold out the Word of life, Jesus, may others know the depth of your love, the richness of your mercy, your unfailing kindness, and your unending grace. May we live out the pages of Scripture and may your words become our own. And Lord, we thank you for all the blessings with which we have been blessed. Help us share these precious, life-changing blessings with others.

In Jesus' name. Amen.

BLESSINGS BEYOND THE PAGE: DAYS 1–20

Day 1 – His word gives us the path.
Day 2 – His word is our guide.
Day 3 – His word gives life.
Day 4 – His word is most valuable.
Day 5 – His word gives us freedom.

Day 6 – His word brings comfort.
Day 7 – His word brings friendship.
Day 8 – His word brings encouragement.
Day 9 – His word brings provision.
Day 10 – His word brings patience.

Day 11 – His word is eternal, enduring.
Day 12 – His word is wisdom.
Day 13 – His word is light.
Day 14 – His word is sustaining grace.
Day 15 – His word is truth.

Day 16 – In His word, we have a wonderful life.
Day 17 – In His word, we have integrity.
Day 18 – In His word, we have confidence.
Day 19 – In His word we have assurance.
Day 20 – In His word, we have joy.

DAY 1

How can a young person stay on the path of purity? By living according to your word.

—Psalm 119:9

The path of the righteous is like the morning sun, shining ever brighter till the full light of day.

—Proverbs 4:18

Teach me, Lord, the way of your decrees, that I may follow it to the end.

—Psalm 119:33

Then you will understand what is right and just and fair—every good path.

—Proverbs 2:9

Trust in the Lord with all your heart and lean not on your own understanding; in all your ways submit to him, and he will make your paths straight.

—Proverbs 3:5–6

DAY 1 – HIS WORD GIVES US THE PATH TO FOLLOW.

Psalm 119:9, Proverbs 4:18, Psalm 119:33, Proverbs 2:9

Daily Precept: Psalm 119:9

Daily Ponder: Proverbs 3:5–6

Day 1 – His Word Gives Us the Path to Follow.

Daily Practice:

Daily Praise:

DAY 1 - HIS WORD GIVES US THE PATH TO FOLLOW.

Daily Progress:

We walk in His ways according to His word—ways of kindness, integrity, generosity. Our words are grace-filled. Our hearts are filled with joy. Our minds are faith-forward. Our thoughts and actions are other-focused in our marriages, in our relationships with our children, friends, and coworkers. We maintain the same approach in our jobs and our encounters with people we meet along the way.

When faced with a trying situation, we do not say, "I trust you Lord, but______." Instead, we say, "I have this _______, but I trust you, Lord." What comes after the "but" is almost always the more important thing, the truth and our focus.

Focus on today, not the past or the future. We say, "Since God is in my tomorrow, I do not fear. Since God redeemed my past, I do not dwell there." Today is the day the Lord has made; let us rejoice and be glad in it. His mercy is for today, and there will more mercy for tomorrow, whatever it may hold. Truly, all we have is today. Live in such a way as to receive his grace and mercy for this day.

Daily Prayer:

> Lord,
>
> Direction and guidance may only come one step at a time, but I know you are in my today and in all my tomorrows. You know the steps I need to take. Give me feet that move and a willing spirit to take one step toward you and then another and another until I am walking in step with you for all my days.
>
> In the name of Jesus, the One who is The Way. Amen.

DAY 2

Your statutes are my delight; they are my counselors.

—Psalm 119:24

I will instruct you and teach you in the way you should go; I will counsel you with my loving eye on you.

—Psalm 32:8

For this God is our God for ever and ever; he will be our guide even to the end.

—Psalm 48:14

But when he, the Spirit of truth comes, he will guide you into all the truth. He will not speak on his own; he will speak only what he hears, and what he will tell you what is yet to come.

—John 16:13

Guide me in your truth and teach me, for you are God my Savior, and my hope is in you all day long.

—Psalm 25:5

DAY 2 – HIS WORD IS OUR GUIDE.

Psalm 119:24, Psalm 32:8, Psalm 48:14, John 16:13

Daily Precept: Psalm 119:24

Daily Ponder: Psalm 25:5

DAY 2 – HIS WORD IS OUR GUIDE.

Daily Practice:

Daily Praise:

DAY 2 – HIS WORD IS OUR GUIDE.

Daily Progress:

What do we give our attention to? We need to give our attention to the best advice, which may sound like this: "Be quick to listen, slow to speak, slow to anger," "Honor your parents," "Do not fear, fret or worry," "Be still and know that I am God," or "Forgive one another just as Christ has forgiven you."

Who do we value as counselors? We need to find those who love God and His word; who are loving, tender, and truthful; and who point us to Jesus. And often, our counselor is the word of God, which comes from the Holy Spirit who is our ultimate counselor and guide.

Following God is a learned behavior. As we learn from the master teacher, our following becomes an act of love because of His love for us. When we follow His word, our guidance is solid, we are not easily swayed, we make time for the important, and we seek God first.

Daily Prayer:

> Lord, we delight in your word because you love us; these are your words— heartfelt, pure, perfect, eternal, and preserved for all time and beyond time. We know your words will never pass away. Thank you for the Spirit's inspiration and the authors' obedience; thank you sending Jesus to fulfill the word, becoming the Word of life. May I not just read but know the why and who behind the words. May I seek your word first, and may those who offer advice, counsel, and guidance also seek and love your word above all.
>
> In the name of Jesus, the One who guides our steps. Amen.

DAY 3

My soul clings to the dust; give me life according to your word!

—Psalm 119:25 ESV

You make known to me the path of life; You will fill me with joy in your presence, with eternal pleasures at your right hand.

—Psalm 16:11

In him was life, and that life was the light of all mankind.

—John 1:4

Then you will shine among them like stars in the sky as you hold firmly to the word of life.

—Philippians 2:15b–16a

Whoever pursues righteousness and love finds life, prosperity and honor.

—Proverbs 21:21

DAY 3 – HIS WORD GIVES LIFE.

Psalm 119:25, Psalm 16:11, John 1:4, Philippians 2:15b–16a

Daily Precept: Psalm 119:25

Daily Ponder: Proverbs 21:21

DAY 3 – HIS WORD GIVES LIFE.

Daily Practice:

Daily Praise:

DAY 3 - HIS WORD GIVES LIFE.

Daily Progress:

God's word is living and active. It never becomes outdated like technology. It doesn't depreciate.

God's word is light and life. When we read it, seek it, follow it, and obey it, we receive blessings of life with a new perspective, and we gain a new purpose filled with opportunities, missions, and ministry.

The psalmist leans even more on God and His promises as he is asking for restoration, revival, and renewal in his life. His example shows us who we should lean on and what we should ask for when life is more than a little messy.

When we feel like we are laid low, wiped out, face-planted on the ground or when we feel like dirt—messy and muddy—we need to remember that the Lord can do a lot with a little dirt (recall Genesis 2:7). In those difficult times, we need to turn it all over to him and let him breathe new life into us through His Spirit.

Daily Prayer:

> Thank you, Lord, that you don't mind my earthiness or my messy, muddy dirt. According to your word, your love reaches to the heavens and into my life. You are high and lifted up, but you will come low to my aid—to give me life, hope, joy, and purpose. Thank you for your word, which is ageless, timeless, living, and active. May it be alive in me.
>
> In the name of Jesus, our life and our light. Amen.

DAY 4

The words you speak to me are worth more than all the riches and wealth in the whole world!

—Psalm 119:72 TPT

Turn my eyes away from worthless things; preserve my life according to your word.

—Psalm 119:37

Wisdom is a gift from a generous God, and every word he speaks is full of revelation and becomes a fountain of understanding within you.

—Proverbs 2:6 TPT

Oh, the depths of the riches of the wisdom and knowledge of God! How unsearchable his judgments, and his path beyond tracing out!

—Romans 11:33

Blessings pour over t he ones who find wisdom, for they have obtained living-understanding. As wisdom increases, a great treasure is imparted, Greater than many bars of refined gold. It is a more valuable commodity than gold and gemstones, for there is nothing you desire that could compare.

—Proverbs 3:13–15 TPT

DAY 4 – HIS WORD IS MOST VALUABLE.

Psalm 119:72, Psalm 119:37, Proverbs 2:6, Romans 11:33

Daily Precept: Psalm 119:72

Daily Ponder: Proverbs 3:13–15

DAY 4 – HIS WORD IS MOST VALUABLE.

Daily Practice:

Daily Praise:

DAY 4 – HIS WORD IS MOST VALUABLE.

Daily Progress:

His word reveals what is valuable, worthy, and precious. Among other things, God values a cheerful giver, gracious speech, knowing Christ, godliness, the unfading beauty of a quiet and gentle spirit, genuine faith, and you and me. See 2 Corinthians 9:7, Proverbs 10:20, Philippians 3:8, 1 Peter 3:4, 1 Peter 1:7, Matthew 10:31, and 1Timothy 4:8.

We find truth in God. He shows me what or who has value. When the world asks me to chase after ________, I need to run after the Lord and his path instead. We need to know that these words from God are for us, personally and collectively. He speaks to our hearts through His word, and His Spirit gives wise counsel.

Daily Prayer:

> Thank you for the blessings poured over my life—eternal blessings, earthly blessings, both visible and invisible blessings. Turn my eyes to what is worthy, valuable, true, and right. May I see you and your word as my treasure and my true riches; help me seek after the things you value. Thank you for valuing me especially when it's hard for me to see my own worth. You bought me with the blood of Jesus and looked beyond to see his beauty in me.
>
> In the name of Jesus, the only One who is worthy. Amen.

DAY 5

I will walk about in freedom, for I have sought out your precepts.

—Psalm 119:45

I have chosen the way of faithfulness; I have set my heart on your laws.

—Psalm 119:30

To the Jews who had believed in him, Jesus said, "If you hold to my teaching, you are really my disciples. Then you will know the truth and the truth will set you free."

—John 8:31–32

Sin is no longer your master, for you no longer live under the requirements of the law. Instead, you live under the freedom of God's grace.

—Romans 6:14 NLT

It is for freedom that Christ has set us free. Stand firm, then, and do not let yourselves be burdened again by the yoke of slavery.

—Galatians 5:1

My friends, you were chosen to be free. So don't use your freedom as an excuse to do anything you want. Use it as an opportunity to serve each other with love.

—Galatians 5:13 CEV

DAY 5 – HIS WORD GIVES US FREEDOM.

Psalm 119:45, Psalm 119:30, John 8:32, Romans 6:14

Daily Precept: Psalm 119:45

Daily Ponder: Galatians 5:1, 13

DAY 5 – HIS WORD GIVES US FREEDOM.

Daily Practice:

Daily Praise:

DAY 5 – HIS WORD GIVES US FREEDOM.

Daily Progress:

Our freedom is to be expressed through love, joy, and more. It is to be a testimony of God's great love for us. With my freedom:

> I can give because I am no longer a slave to greed.
> I can serve because I am longer a slave to status.
> I can praise because I am no longer a slave to despair.
> I can love because I am no longer a slave to self.
> I can __________because I am no longer a slave to ___________.

Love is our motivation because the only thing that counts is faith expressing itself through love. We have been set free, so we can love as Jesus does. We are set free from the law of sin and death—we walk in the way of Love with confidence, assurance, and gratitude.

Daily Prayer:

> Thank you, Lord, for this freedom—the wide, roomy space where your love has brought me. Your grace fills this space. Let me be reminded that I am no longer a slave to fear, worry, regret, shame, or condemnation. Put me back on your path of freedom, of faith in Jesus where there is no condemnation but only love, forgiveness, acceptance, belonging, and more —wide open spaces of your deep love and abiding presence.
>
> In the name of Jesus, the Good Shepherd, who leads to green pastures of grace. Amen.

DAY 6

I find true comfort, Lord, because your laws have stood the test of time.

—Psalm 119:52 CEV

When I am hurting, I find comfort in your promise that leads to life.

—Psalm 119:50 CEV

The LORD *is close to the brokenhearted and saves those who are crushed in spirit.*

—Psalm 34:18

When anxiety was great within me, your consolation brought me joy.

—Psalm 94:19

Praise be to the God and Father of our Lord Jesus Christ, the Father of compassion and the God of all comfort, who comforts us in all our troubles, so that we can comfort those in any trouble with the comfort we ourselves receive from God.

—2 Corinthians 1:3–4

DAY 6 – HIS WORD BRINGS COMFORT.

Psalm 119:52, Psalm 119:50, Psalm 34:18, Psalm 94:19

Daily Precept: Psalm 119:50

Daily Ponder: 2 Corinthians 1:3–4

DAY 6 - HIS WORD BRINGS COMFORT.

Daily Practice:

Daily Praise:

DAY 6 – HIS WORD BRINGS COMFORT.

Daily Progress:

The psalmist asks to be revived in the fullness of life in God's favor and grace through the promises in His word. You may get the impression that he has already asked for this. Be assured that he has. This lets us know that our requests are not just one and done. We can ask and seek God's favor over and over again. He never tires of us! Our troubles, sufferings, afflictions, and sorrows may not be removed, but we are given promises. We are revived and strengthened through His word, and we are being led to life and peace.

We need to watch out for those who want us to linger in misery because misery loves company. Rather, we need to look for those who will lift us out of misery.

In times of difficulty, we can ask, "Why?" But to dwell there will create doubts and more despair. It's better to ask, "Who can I help in their time of need? Lord, what am I learning from you in this situation?" Or say, "Lord, show me how to lean on you when I cannot even find the strength to stand."

Daily Prayer:

> Lord, your promises lead me to life, hope, peace, and assurance. You give me comfort to weather all troubles; hope to endure; love to propel me forward; grace to remain; faith to move mountains (of misery of sorrow); gifts of power, love, and self-discipline; promises to remember; words to recite; life in Jesus; love; compassion; and presence. Where you are, there is love and light, the hope of heaven, joy in each day, and blessings beyond the page.
>
> In the name of Jesus, the One who comforts us. Amen.

DAY 7

I am a friend to all who fear you, to all who follow your precepts.

—Psalm 119:63

The righteous choose their friends carefully, but the way of the wicked leads them astray.

—Proverbs 12:26

Do not make friends with a hot-tempered person, do not associate with one easily angered, or you may learn their ways and get yourself ensnared.

—Proverbs 22:24–25

You are my friends if you do what I command.

—John 15:14

Be devoted to one another in love. Honor one another above yourselves.

—Romans 12:10

DAY 7 - HIS WORD BRINGS FRIENDSHIP.

Psalm 119:63, Proverbs12:26, Proverbs 22:24, John 15:14

Daily Precept: Psalm 119:63

Daily Ponder: Romans 12:10

DAY 7 – HIS WORD BRINGS FRIENDSHIP.

Daily Practice:

Daily Praise:

DAY 7 – HIS WORD BRINGS FRIENDSHIP.

Daily Progress:

God's word guides me in my choice of relationships—spouse, friends, associates, and acquaintances. We need to ask, "Are my friends, friends with God?" To walk in the daily and live for Jesus, we need friends who walk with and live for Jesus daily. My friends will be God's friends too.

If there are those who do not know or believe in Jesus, we are to be witnesses of the love and kindness of Jesus, the grace of God as well as the forgiveness and salvation from God.

We draw wisdom, gain strength, receive good advice, and find help from those whose friendship with Jesus is at the center of their lives. We want to have complete commitment to God and His word, even in our friendships!

Daily Prayer:

> Thank you, Lord, for a deep abiding presence, dwelling in my life and in my heart. Thank you that you have called me friend. Thank you for the gift of friendship with you, Father, and with Jesus and with those who love you and are your friends too. May we seek to have friendships that draw us closer to you, as we learn to love one another as you have done for us. Jesus, you are our perfect friend who will always be with us and never forsake us— may we invite you to be in all our relationships.
>
> In the name of Jesus, the One who calls us friend. Amen.

DAY 8

Your extravagant kindness to me makes me want to follow your words even more!

—Psalm 119:65 TPT

But those who hope in the Lord *will renew their strength. They will soar on wings like eagles; they will run and not grow weary, they will walk and not be faint.*

—Isaiah 40:31

May the God who gives endurance and encouragement give you the same attitude and mind toward each other that that Christ Jesus had.

—Romans 15:5

Preach the word; be prepared in season and out of season; correct, rebuke and encourage—with great patience and careful instruction.

—2 Timothy 4:2

May our Lord Jesus Christ himself and God our Father, who loved us and by his grace gave us eternal encouragement and good hope, encourage your hearts and strengthen you in every good deed and word.

—2 Thessalonians 2:16–17

Day 8 – His Word Brings Encouragement.

Psalm 119:65, Isaiah 40:31, Romans 15:5, 2 Timothy 4:2

Daily Precept: Psalm 119:65

Daily Ponder: 2 Thessalonians 2:16–17

DAY 8 – HIS WORD BRINGS ENCOURAGEMENT.

Daily Practice:

Daily Praise:

DAY 8 – HIS WORD BRINGS ENCOURAGEMENT.

Daily Progress:

We are learning all the time and exposed to so many things. Who or where do we get encouragement from? And does it point us to God-things or to self-things? We must believe that God is an encourager, not a discourager. God cheers us on; He gives us courage for the next time; He gives us endurance to try again—to take the next step in faith (Romans 15:5).

Be in the word daily. He gives us what we need each day—a gentle answer, an apt reply, listening ears, wise lips, a cheerful heart, and the list goes on. His extravagant kindness causes us to be devoted to one another and to doing what is good (Titus 3:1–8).

Daily Prayer:

> Thank you for your words; they are the words of life, even though some may be hard to hear and even harder to do. Let us be encouraged by the confidence and strength you provide through your word and through Jesus. You have given us all that we need to do all that you have asked us to do. May our hearts be encouraged as you are our eternal encourager.
>
> In the name of Jesus, the word of Life. Amen.

DAY 9

Your hands made me and established me; Give me understanding and a teachable heart, that I may learn Your commands.

—Psalm 119:73 AMP

The Lord is my shepherd, I lack nothing.

—Psalm 23:1

You have searched me, Lord, and you know me.

—Psalm 139:1

And my God will meet all your needs according to the riches of his glory in Christ Jesus.

—Philippians 4:19

And God will generously provide all you need. Then you will always have everything you need, and plenty left over to share with others.

—2 Corinthians 9:8 NLT

DAY 9 – HIS WORD BRINGS PROVISION.

Psalm 119:73, Psalm 23:1, Psalm 139:1, Philippians 4:19

Daily Precept: Psalm 119:73

Daily Ponder: 2 Corinthians 9:8

DAY 9 – HIS WORD BRINGS PROVISION.

Daily Practice:

Daily Praise:

DAY 9 – HIS WORD BRINGS PROVISION.

Daily Progress:

His word teaches us how to use our body, mind, time, talents, and money. His word teaches us how to be a friend and how to treat friends, strangers, enemies, and authorities. His word teaches us how to have healthy marriages, how to raise children, and how to teach others and have work-life balance.

His word teaches us how to make right decisions; it warns about what happens when we make wrong choices and shows us the way to turn back. His word teaches us how to give and receive, share and accept, be content, and be grateful. He supplies our every need in every area of our life.

Daily Prayer:

> Lord, whether in plenty or in want, famine or feast, joy or sorrow, victory or defeat, you have met us with everything we need; all we need is you. You have supplied us generously with your love, grace, mercy, kindness, salvation, forgiveness, and your provision. You lavish your love on us with fresh mercy every morning. You do not leave us empty, even when we share and give—especially when we share and give. May we give above and beyond in every opportunity, for you have prepared blessings for us as we go and give, teach and share, live and serve.
>
> In the name of Jesus, the One who supplies all our needs. Amen.

DAY 10

In your unfailing love preserve my life, that I may obey the statutes of your mouth.

—Psalm 119:88

Be still before the Lord *and wait patiently for him; do not fret when people succeed in their ways, when they carry out wicked schemes.*

—Psalm 37:7

Be joyful in hope, patient in affliction, faithful in prayer.

—Romans 12:12

You need to persevere so that when you have done the will of God, you will receive what he has promised.

—Hebrews 10:36

I remain confident of this: I will see the goodness of the Lord *in the land of the living. Wait for the* Lord*; be strong and take heart and wait for the* Lord*.*

—Psalm 27:13–14

DAY 10 – HIS WORD BRINGS PATIENCE.

Psalm 119:88, Psalm 37:7, Romans 12:12, Hebrews 10:36

Daily Precept: Psalm 119:88

Daily Ponder: Psalm 27:13–14

DAY 10 – HIS WORD BRINGS PATIENCE.

Daily Practice:

Daily Praise:

DAY 10 – HIS WORD BRINGS PATIENCE.

Daily Progress:

The psalmist asks for preservation. The preserving process is the best way to keep fresh produce at its very best. In the same way, God's unfailing love is the best way to keep us for His best, so that we may witness to others of God's presence and His goodness, even as we wait for answers to prayer.

Cultivate a waiting rhythm. While you are waiting for an answer, you can:

1. Pray with questions: When? How long? What am I learning?
2. Seek Scripture that you use as a mantra while waiting.
3. Ask godly advisors and friends to pray for you.
4. Pray with intention: "Lord, in the waiting, I know you will work_________; let me wait patiently without complaining."
5. Give your attention to others who need help and encouragement. You may be the help that God uses to answer another's prayer while you wait.
6. Focus your attitude on keeping His word.
7. Repeat these steps as many times as needed. Pray, seek, ask, give, focus, repeat.

We can see God's presence in this life —we need to look for it, and we need to know what His goodness looks like.

Daily Prayer:

> Lord, in the waiting, help us to believe that you are love, that you are working from a place of love, that you will answer from a place of love, and that your word is love spoken. You demonstrate your love to us in that while

we were sinners, Christ came. And now as we develop patience through seasons of waiting, may we seek your word, remain in your word, and hold onto the words promised—promises of your faithfulness.

In the name of Jesus, the One who invites us to come and rest in the waiting. Amen.

DAY 11

Your word, LORD, is eternal; it stands firm in the heavens.

—Psalm 119:89

Long ago I learned from your statutes that you established them to last forever.

—Psalm 119:152

I keep the LORD in mind always. Because He is at my right hand, I will not be shaken.

—Psalm 16:8 HCSB

Heaven and earth will pass away but my words will never pass away.

—Matthew 24:35

The earth and everything in it, the world and its inhabitants, belong to the LORD; for He laid the foundations on the seas and established it on the rivers.

—Psalm 24:1–2 HCSB

DAY 11 – HIS WORD IS ETERNAL, ENDURING.

Psalm 119:89, Psalm 119:52, Psalm 16:8, Matthew 24:35

Daily Precept: Psalm 119:89

Daily Ponder: Psalm 24:1–2

DAY 11 – HIS WORD IS ETERNAL, ENDURING.

Daily Practice:

Daily Praise:

DAY 11 – HIS WORD IS ETERNAL, ENDURING.

Daily Progress:

We can have stability because His word is our foundation, and Jesus, the Word, is our cornerstone. Because His word stands forever, we can stand firm in His love and truth and in Jesus, the Word of Life.

When we walk in the light of His presence and have the living, enduring word, we can be a light, a sure thing for those around us:

> We can be the calm in the chaos.
> We can have joy in the midst of sorrow.
> We can bring truth to confusion.
> We can bring generosity because we know who owns everything.

We become stewards when we realize He is the Owner of everything. The earth is full of His glory, and we can tend to this earth to bear witness to the goodness of God.

Daily Prayer:

> Thank you, Jesus! You turn my night into day, my worry into worship, and my fear into faith. You cause my wobbly heart to remain steadfast. You are my foundation; your word stands firm in the heavens and are fastened to eternity; therefore, I can stand upon the solid rock, knowing that your word endures.
>
> In the name of Jesus, the Rock on which I stand. Amen.

DAY 12

Your commands are always with me and make me wiser than my enemies.

—Psalm 119:98

For the Lord *gives wisdom; from his mouth come knowledge and understanding.*

—Proverbs 2:6

If any of you lacks wisdom, you should ask God, who gives generously to all without finding fault, and it [*wisdom*] *will be given to you.*

—James 1:5

Who is wise and understanding among you? Let them show it by their good life and, by deeds done in the humility that comes from wisdom.

—James 3:13

I have not departed from your laws, for you yourself have taught me. How sweet are your words to my taste, sweeter than honey to my mouth!

—Psalm 119:102–103

DAY 12 – HIS WORD IS WISDOM.

Psalm 119:98, Proverbs 2:6, James 1:5, James 3:13

Daily Precept: Psalm 119:98

Daily Ponder: Psalm 119:102–103

Day 12 – His Word Is Wisdom.

Daily Practice:

Daily Praise:

DAY 12 - HIS WORD IS WISDOM.

Daily Progress:

God's word gives us things to think on—things to set our minds upon. We gain wisdom, insight, discernment, and understanding through knowing, seeking, studying, meditating, obeying, and loving God and His word.

God's wisdom is pure, peace-loving, considerate, submissive, full of mercy and good fruit, impartial and sincere. When we follow God's word, we build a strong foundation, and our wisdom, insights, discernment, and understanding need to look and act like His.

We have been anointed [given a special endowment] with the truth from Jesus (1 John 2:20, 27). Our hearts must be open and teachable especially when it comes to difficult truths.

Daily Prayer:

> Lord, when difficult truths come, give us wisdom and a desire to obey, for we know that they are truths from your word. They are holy and perfect, written with a perfect love and a perfect will. Let us obey boldly and speak graciously to those who need to hear the truth—even truths that we also need to hear.
>
> In the precious and perfect name of Jesus. Amen.

DAY 13

Your word is a lamp for my feet, a light on my path.

—Psalm 119:105

You, LORD, are my lamp; the LORD turns my darkness into light.

—2 Samuel 22:29

For this command is a lamp, this teaching is a light, and correction and instruction are the way of life.

—Proverbs 6:23

When Jesus spoke again to the people, he said, "I am the light of the world. Whoever follows me will never walk in darkness, but will have the light of life."

—John 8:12

"You are the light of the world. A town built on a hill cannot be hidden . . . . In the same way, let your light shine before others that they may see your good deeds and glorify your Father in heaven."

—Matthew 5:14, 16

DAY 13 – HIS WORD IS LIGHT.

Psalm 119:105, 2 Samuel 22:29, Proverbs 6:23, John 8:12

Daily Precept: Psalm 119:105

Daily Ponder: Matthew 5:14, 16

DAY 13 – HIS WORD IS LIGHT.

Daily Practice:

Daily Praise:

DAY 13 - HIS WORD IS LIGHT.

Daily Progress:

When we allow God's word to be our guide and illuminate our course of life, we gain understanding. God's word gives light; we have to study, meditate, and obey it.

When Jesus, the Word of life, makes an entrance, we are moved from darkness to light because He is the Light. The Father has given us the perfect light, Jesus. Daily, we need His word as our light and lamp; turn and learn more of Jesus. All our good points to the goodness of God.

Daily Prayer:

> Thank you, Lord, that our next step with you is always in the light —even if that is all we know, one step in the light at a time. Lord, help us, guide us, and teach us to let your word glisten and illuminate our course of life. Remind us, Lord, that loving your word, following your word, and trusting the Word of life build the foundation of our life. Let Jesus, the light of the world, be reflected in us.
>
> In the name of Jesus, the Light of Life. Amen.

DAY 14

Sustain me, my God, according to your promise, and I will live; Do not let my hopes be dashed.

—Psalm 119:116

Let me live that I may praise you, and may your laws sustain me.

—Psalm 119:175

Let me again experience the joy of your deliverance. Sustain me by giving me the desire to obey.

—Psalm 51:12 NET

Even to your old age and gray hairs, I am he, I am he who will sustain you. I have made you and I will carry you; I will sustain you and I will rescue you.

—Isaiah 46:4

The Sovereign LORD *has given me a well-instructed tongue, to know the word that sustains the weary. He wakens me morning by morning, wakens my ear to listen like one being instructed.*

—Isaiah 50:4

DAY 14 – HIS WORD IS SUSTAINING GRACE.

Psalm 119:116, Psalm 119:175, Psalm 51:12, Isaiah 46:4

Daily Precept: Psalm 119:116

Daily Ponder: Isaiah 50:4 or Isaiah 46:4

DAY 14 – HIS WORD IS SUSTAINING GRACE.

Daily Practice:

Daily Praise:

DAY 14 – HIS WORD IS SUSTAINING GRACE.

Daily Progress:

We find sustaining grace in His word, in His promises, and in our obedience. We know the word that sustains us, and our response is to listen.

His very words tell of His sustaining grace:

> He made us.
> He loves us.
> He will carry us.
> He will rescue us.
> He will wake us and our listening ears to His word.
> He will teach us.
> He will be with us.

When we are weary, He gives us rest, renewal, restoration—grace (Psalm 51:12).

Daily Prayer:

> Thank you, Lord, that your grace is sufficient. It is truly all we need—your divine unmerited favor given to us at just the right time. How truly generous and compassionate you are—bestowing common grace to all whether they know you or not. You provide the food, water, air, nature, beauty, friendship, and more good things we experience because all good gifts are from you. Those who believe in you, Jesus, receive saving grace —forgiveness, freedom, the hope of heaven, light, truth, and your unending love. Saving grace brings the great things of God. And

sustaining grace brings fresh and new mercies every morning—compassion that never fails. You restore our soul, refresh our spirit, and fill our lives with good things that we do not deserve though your love pours them out on us. Give us grace for the moment so that our moment will be yours.

In the name of Jesus, who is our grace. Amen.

DAY 15

My eyes strain to see your rescue, to see the truth of your promise fulfilled.

—Psalm 119:123 NLT

All your words are true; all your righteous laws are eternal.

—Psalm 119:160

Buy the truth and do not sell it—wisdom, instruction and insight as well.

—Proverbs 23:23

Jesus answered, "I am the way and the truth and the life. No one comes to the Father except through me."

—John 14:6

Instead, speaking the truth in love, we will grow to become in every respect the mature body of him who is the head, that is, Christ.

—Ephesians 4:15

DAY 15 – HIS WORD IS TRUTH.

Psalm 119:123, Psalm 119:160, Proverbs 23:23, John 14:6

Daily Precept: Psalm 119:123

Daily Ponder: Ephesians 4:15

DAY 15 – HIS WORD IS TRUTH.

Daily Practice:

Daily Praise:

DAY 15 – HIS WORD IS TRUTH.

Daily Progress:

God's word is changeless, timeless, living, and active. The sum of all Scripture is the truth, our foundation. Jesus is our foundation as He is the way, the truth and the life. We cannot have the Bible plus _________. We must hold everything up to the truth of God's word.

As we gain wisdom from His word, we will know when it is better to give an apt reply, be slow to speak, or remain silent. When we speak truth, we do so with the intention of bringing those who do not know the truth to the One who is truth and love.

There is truth, and there are preferences, opinions, and beliefs. As followers of Jesus, we speak the truth (the gospel) in love, and our preferences, opinions, and beliefs align with the word of God. As we come to know His word, we speak—not legalistically but lovingly—because we know His way, His will, and His word. His word is truth, the perfect answer to all of life's questions.

Daily Prayer:

> Lord, in a world of half-truths, relative truth, almost truths, and no truth, help us know your word, which is true and right. And help us understand and know that Jesus is the truth, the way, and the life. Thank you that the truth on the pages of Scripture will set us free from the lies of the enemy. We want to live by every word that comes from you so that our love and faith can increase. Help us to share the truth of the cross and the truth of your grace.
>
> In the name of Jesus, the One who is truth and love. Amen.

DAY 16

Your statutes are wonderful; therefore, I obey them.

—Psalm 119:129

Many, LORD, my God, are the wonders you have done, the things you planned for us. None can compare with you; were I to speak and tell of your deeds, they would be too many to declare.

—Psalm 40:5

All this also comes from the LORD Almighty, whose plan is wonderful, whose wisdom is magnificent.

—Isaiah 28:29

I praise you because I am fearfully and wonderfully made; your works are wonderful, I know that full well.

—Psalm 139:14

Open my eyes that I may see wonderful things in your law.

—Psalm 119:18

DAY 16 – IN HIS WORD, WE HAVE A WONDERFUL LIFE.

Psalm 119:129, Psalm 40:5, Isaiah 28:29, Psalm 139:14

Daily Precept: Psalm 119:129

Daily Ponder: Psalm 119:18

Day 16 – In His Word, We Have a Wonderful Life.

Daily Practice:

Daily Praise:

DAY 16 – IN HIS WORD, WE HAVE A WONDERFUL LIFE.

Daily Progress:

We not only see His wonder in the Wow moments, but we also have to see His wonder in the Now moments. To see wonderful things, we have to be looking for the wonderful in all things.

Even when we struggle to see beyond our circumstance, we know that He has done wonderful things. This is a starter list; add more entries as wonderful things are brought to mind:

> He provides our daily needs.
> He is faithful.
> He hears us and is close to the brokenhearted.
> He has given us redemption and a covenant.
> He has given us the hope and home of heaven.
> His word is right, true, and enduring.

Daily Prayer:

> Lord, we praise you for the miraculous signs and wonders that you have performed for us. Daily, you meet us where we are with the blessings that we need. Moment by moment, your wonders declare the beauty of this world. We ask for sight to see the wonders in our life in the ordinary days you make extraordinary—when our home becomes a haven, our job becomes a mission, our meals become food for the soul and body, our words become worship, and our lives become a testimony of your wonderful light, Jesus. May we see the wonderful life you have given us.
>
> In the name of the one who is wonderful, Jesus. Amen.

DAY 17

You are righteous, LORD, and your laws are right.

—Psalm 119:137

Your promises have been thoroughly tested, and your servant loves them.

—Psalm 119:140

Whoever walks in integrity walks securely, but whoever takes crooked paths will be found out.

—Proverbs 10:9

May integrity and uprightness protect me, because my hope, LORD, is in you.

—Psalm 25:21

And whatever you do, whether in word or deed, do it all in the name of the Lord Jesus, giving thanks to God the Father through him.

—Colossians 3:17

DAY 17 – IN HIS WORD, WE HAVE INTEGRITY.

Psalm 119:137, Psalm 119:140, Proverbs 10:9, Psalm 25:21

Daily Precept: Psalm 119:137

Daily Ponder: Colossians 3:17

Day 17 – In His Word, We Have Integrity.

Daily Practice:

Daily Praise:

DAY 17 – IN HIS WORD, WE HAVE INTEGRITY.

Daily Progress:

Our view of God's word impacts how we live out His word. We center our hearts on His word, take our thoughts captive and test them with the truth; we hold onto His teaching and stand firm with His word as our foundation.

We are to be people guided by God's principles, for they bring wholeness and prosperity. When we follow God's word, we are complete; we find that we are to be trustworthy and honest—people of ethics and morality.

In all that we do, we do it for the Lord. We do it for His name. We do it for a higher purpose and with a grateful heart. We want all that we do to point to Jesus.

Daily Prayer:

> Lord, give us a clear view, one that loves your word, delights in your word, trusts and meditates on your word. As the psalmist knew that your word is right, sure, thoroughly tested, everlasting, and righteous, let us know these same truths deep within us. Give us a complete and whole picture of your word, so that we find fullness and abundance and a foundation not made of sand but of the rock of your word—a foundation on which we will not be shaken or unsure. Your word brings honesty and integrity into our lives. May we be ambassadors of Jesus so that others see that you are righteous in all your ways and that you are loving toward all you have made.
>
> In the name of Jesus, the rock on which we stand. Amen.

DAY 18

Long ago I learned from your statutes that you established them to last forever.

—Psalm 119:152

For you have been my hope, Sovereign Lord, *my confidence since my youth.*

—Psalm 71:5

But blessed is the one who trusts in the Lord, *whose confidence is in Him.*

—Jeremiah 17:7

This is the confidence we have in approaching God: that if we ask anything according to his will, he hears us.

—1 John 5:14

I rise before dawn and cry for help; I have put my hope in your word. My eyes stay open through the watches of the night, that I may meditate on your promises.

—Psalm 119:147–148

DAY 18 - IN HIS WORD, WE HAVE CONFIDENCE.

Psalm 119:152, Psalm 71:5, Jeremiah 17:7, 1 John 5:14

Daily Precept: Psalm 119:152

Daily Ponder: Psalm 119:147–148

Day 18 – In His Word, We Have Confidence.

Daily Practice:

Daily Praise:

DAY 18 – IN HIS WORD, WE HAVE CONFIDENCE.

Daily Progress:

God's word is true and established. We gain confidence through His word and His work for us (Philippians 1:6). Through faith in Jesus, we can approach God with freedom and confidence (Ephesians 3:12).

You and I need a holy rhythm in our day. Morning and evening our hearts, our words, our thoughts, our hope need to be in His word. We rise and pray; we lie down and meditate. Create a daily rhythm. Find what works for you. It is never too late to have a lifetime with God!

Daily Prayer:

> Lord, we know that we can pray the word of God to the heart of God. We know that we can come before you with confidence drawing near to you as you are near to us. We thank you for the confidence we receive through Jesus so that we can enter where you are and receive your mercy and grace. And Lord as we know more of your word, let us pray more, ask more, and seek more of you, for there is much we need to learn and many we need to love. Thank you that we can know you, trust you, and trust your word. We ask all things without arrogance or pride but confidently with the assurance that you will hear us and work all things for our good and your glory.
>
> In the name of the One who is our confidence, Jesus. Amen.

DAY 19

Your compassion, LORD, is great; preserve my life according to your laws.

—Psalm 119:156

For no word from God will ever fail.

—Luke 1:37

And my God will meet all your needs according to the riches of his glory in Christ Jesus.

—Philippians 4:16

And so we know and rely on the love of God has for us. God is love. Whoever lives in love lives in God, and God in them.

—I John 4:19

The steadfast love of the LORD never ceases; his mercies never come to an end; they are new every morning; great is your faithfulness. "The LORD is my portion," says my soul, "therefore I will hope in him."

—Lamentations 3:22–24 ESV

DAY 19 – IN HIS WORD, WE HAVE ASSURANCE.

Psalm 119:156, Luke 1:37, Philippians 4:16, 1 John 4:19

Daily Precept: Psalm 119:156

Daily Ponder: Lamentations 3:22–24

DAY 19 – IN HIS WORD, WE HAVE ASSURANCE.

Daily Practice:

Daily Praise:

DAY 19 – IN HIS WORD, WE HAVE ASSURANCE.

Daily Progress:

He will defend, redeem, and preserve us according to His promises, His word, and His love.

Compassion and grace go hand in hand; the Lord meets us with compassion and grace. Our assurance is that even when we fail Him, He will not fail us. His word will not fail, and His love will not fail.

When lies creep in with whispers or shouts of condemnation, guilt, or shame, turn to His word and find encouragement such as this in Romans: "Therefore, there is no condemnation for those who are in Christ Jesus, because through Christ Jesus the law of the Spirit who gives life has set you free" (Romans 8:1–2, Romans 8:31–39). This is the voice we should listen to!

Daily Prayer:

> Thank you, Lord, for who you are and who I am in you. You look upon me with perfect love and compassion that is tender and kind. You desire for me to do your will because you know the plans you have for me. You know my comings and goings, when I lie down and when I rise. We have new mercies every morning, peaceful sleep at night, and the grace upon grace you lavish on us daily. We rely on your word and the love you have for us, and we know that your love will never fail. You will never fail, and your word will never fail. I have this blessed assurance that you, Jesus, are mine and I am yours—what a foretaste of glory divine! Thank you!
>
> In the name of Jesus, the One who is our blessed assurance. Amen.

DAY 20

Your promises are the source of my bubbling joy; the revelation of your Word thrills me like one who has discovered hidden treasure.

—Psalm 119:162 TPT

Fill my heart with joy when their grain and new wine abound.

—Psalm 4:7

Rejoice in the Lord always. I will say it again: Rejoice!

—Philippians 4:4

Rejoice always, pray continually, give thanks in all circumstances; for this is God's will for you in Christ Jesus.

—1 Thessalonians 5:16–18

The Lord *is my strength and my shield; my heart trusts in him, and he helps me. My heart leaps for joy, and with my song I praise him.*

—Psalm 28:7

DAY 20 – IN HIS WORD, WE HAVE JOY.

Psalm 119:162, Psalm 4:7, Philippians 4:4, 1 Thessalonians 5:16–18

Daily Precept: Psalm 119:162

Daily Ponder: Psalm 28:7

Day 20 – In His Word, We Have Joy.

Daily Practice:

Daily Praise:

DAY 20 – IN HIS WORD, WE HAVE JOY.

Daily Progress:

We have come across the great and unexpected treasure of God's word. Our hearts are strengthened by grace. Our lives are transformed when we are in the word, and the more we know Jesus through His word, the more we become like Him.

When others succeed, we can be filled with joy because our story and our success are not dependent on theirs. We trust the Lord for His plan for us. How do we fill our hearts with joy? What do we put in our hearts? His word, His Spirit, His promises, His hope, and His love. We trust in His promises and His word to bring joy and peace. We find joy in being with His people.

When it is hard to praise, know that praise can be a sacrifice (Hebrews 13:15). Sometimes, it is easier to keep quiet or to go along with complainers, gossipers, lamenters, worriers, and arguers. But praise is something we offer to God, and it brings gratitude into our hearts. Without praise, joy cannot be expressed.

Daily Prayer:

> Lord, we rejoice in your promise, as one who has found the spoils of war. When your word fills our hearts, joy fills our worship, our words, and our works. You fill us with joy and peace as we trust you. You hold nothing back; you are generous and good to us. May our hearts pour out your praise with gratitude and thanksgiving knowing that your promises bring life, peace, understanding, truth, assurance, the wonderful joy that is found in Jesus, and so much more.
>
> In the name of Jesus, the joy of our heart. Amen.

DAILY LIVING

1. How does His word guide you in your relationships? In your finances? In your decisions? Do you see an area that needs more of His guidance and less self-reliance?

2. Where do you see opportunities for patience? How can you reframe annoyances and disruptions as "patience planters"?

3. Knowing that His word is eternal and enduring, how does that increase your confidence when you face the inconsistency of the world?

4. When His word fills our hearts, joy fills our words and our works. With assurance of His promises, how do you make the joy of the Lord evident to others?

FINDING HIS WORD FOR ANSWERS IN EVERYDAY LIFE

Here are a few Scriptures that can help us deepen our walk, direct our steps, and delight our hearts. Read, study, and then go and do. As you do so, blessings will follow and flow for you and for those around you.

The Beatitudes: Matthew 5, 6, 7 and Luke 6
The Ten Commandments: Exodus 20
Life in the Spirit and doing good to all: Galatians 5, 6
Living as God's children: Ephesians 4, 5, 6
Our thought life: Philippians 4
Wisdom for our every day: Proverbs 1–31 (read one chapter a day)
Our calling: 1 Thessalonians 5:16–18
Rules and instructions for holy living: Colossians 3–4
Practical words for practical living God's way: James 1–5
Our living hope and holy living: 1 Peter 1–5

MORE FROM PSALM 119...

We have...

Calm in chaos
Peace in persecution
Hope in hard times
Delight through the disappointments
Joy amid sorrow
Assurance in uncertainty
Faith in times of doubt

We have …

> Assurance of His compassion, new every morning
> Assurance of His promises, ever faithful
> Assurance of His love, unending

We have…
Promises of hope, life, peace. Here are a few of the treasures we can take hold of:

His word says:

Be not afraid	Cast all our cares on Him.
Be strong	His grace is sufficient.
I am with you	He walks with me.
I will never forsake you	He has a table prepared for me.
I am faithful	He fills me with good things.
His word is good	He is the God of all comfort.
I will never leave you	Our troubles are momentary.

The Spirit gives power, love, and self-discipline.
He works all things for my good and His glory.
There is goodness in the land of the living.
He is the Way and the Truth and the Life.

CONCLUSION

As we come to the end of our study, the blessings continue. Psalm 119 contains many more blessings than the 20 we studied. There are blessings of purity, hope, righteousness, daily study, and balance—just to name a few. As we allow His word to be our guide; create our path; find life and freedom; experience comfort, friendship, and encouragement; we will walk in light, in truth, and in grace. With integrity and confidence, there is nothing that will shake our assurance of all that is to come. Joy-filled and enduring, His word will point us to the Way and the Truth and the Life—Jesus! And when we encounter the Word made flesh, life is truly wonderful.

This is why we want to know His word. His blessings flow as we open our hearts to the words on the pages of Scripture.

Blessings to you as you dig deeper into His Word.

ACKNOWLEDGMENTS

To you, the reader. Thank you for opening the pages of this book and trusting me to share God, His love, and His word with you. May you and I walk in blessings as we hide and treasure His word in our hearts.

To the wonderful team at Lucid Books, I am so thankful for your wisdom, direction, and patience with this first-time author. The Lord has been the center of all that we have done together. What an amazing experience!

To Bob Goff and Kimberly Stewart, your words of affirmation were a gift that spoke into my writing and into my heart. Thank you for giving me the courage to take the next steps.

To the amazing, wise, women who come and open up the word of God with me every Thursday night. My home and heart are filled with the most beautiful gifts of friendship and love. You indulge my creative endeavors and my trial recipes and listen to the oft repeated phrase, "Just another thought for this day." Thank you for allowing me to walk alongside y'all!

To my friends and my family who have encouraged me all along the way, embracing whatever I was working on and always pointing me to our eternal encourager, Jesus.

To my mother, who has always believed in me, in my words, and in my work. She has encouraged me to pursue all things creative and, in all things, the Lord. You have known me before I knew myself. Your words of love and encouragement have been a catalyst in my life. Thank you for walking with me as I found my way.

To my children, Morgan, Savannah, and Presleigh. You are my delight and joy; I have enjoyed every moment of being your mom. From the first steps to the first steps of faith, I have loved walking with you. Keep walking with the Lord—He has amazing things in store for you. I love you with all my heart.

To my husband, Scott, you have loved me for more than half of my life. You know me better than anyone (except the Lord) and have taken all things in stride. Our steps are in sync; we walk in the same direction, and the path He has given us is beautiful. Thank you for asking the important question. . . . I am so glad I said, "Yes." I love you with all my heart.

To the most important person in my life, Jesus, the One who speaks life and love, who rescues and redeems, who writes His name on my heart and my name on His hand. He walks with me even when I run ahead, and when I lag behind, He waits for me on the path, allows me to catch up and guides my steps. Jesus, you are the greatest blessing beyond the pages of Scripture. May I stay close to Your word and walk with you all the days of my life.

PSALM 119

The intention and attention of this Psalm is one that continues to inspire us as we see the details. In each section the title is a letter of the Hebrew alphabet and that in each section, the beginning word in each verse begins with the corresponding letter. Let us remember that every stroke of the pen and every letter of every word is Holy Spirit inspired and is there for us to learn more and to love more.

ᵓALEPH. [א]

1 ᵓašrê t̠əmîmê-d̠ā́rek̠
hạhōlk̠îm bət̠ôrat̠ yhwh(ᵓăd̠ōnāy)

Happy are they that are upright in the way,
who walk in the law of the LORD.

2 ᵓašrê nōṣrê ᶜēd̠ōt̠āyw
bək̠ol-lēb̠ yid̠rəšû́hû

Happy are they that keep His testimonies,
that seek Him with the whole heart.

3 ᵓap̄ lọᵓ-p̄āᶜălû ᶜawlāʰ
bid̠rāk̠āyw hālā́k̠û

Yea, they do no unrighteousness;
they walk in His ways.

4 ᵓattāʰ ṣiwwî́t̠āʰ p̄iqqūd̠eʸ́k̠ā
lišmōr məᵓōd̠

Thou hast ordained Thy precepts,
that we should observe them diligently.

5 ᵓaḥălay yikkṓnû d̠ərāk̠āy
lišmōr ḥuqqeʸ́k̠ā

Oh that my ways were directed
to observe Thy statutes!

6 ᵓāz lōᵓ-ᵓēb̠ôš
bəhabbîṭî ᵓel-kol-miṣwōt̠eʸ́k̠ā

Then should I not be ashamed,
when I have regard unto all Thy commandments.

7 ᵓôd̠k̠ā bəyṓšer lēb̠āb̠
bəlomd̠î mišpəṭê ṣid̠qék̠ā

I will give thanks unto Thee with uprightness of heart,
when I learn Thy righteous ordinances.

8 ᵓet̠-ḥuqqeʸ́k̠ā ᵓešmōr
ᵓạl-taᶜazb̠ḗnî ᶜad̠-məᵓōd̠

I will observe Thy statutes;
O forsake me not utterly. {P}

BETH. [ב]

9 bammeʰ yəzakkeʰ-nnaᶜar ᵓet̠-ᵓorḥô
lišmōr kid̠b̠āréḵā

Wherewithal shall a young man keep his way pure?
By taking heed thereto according to Thy word.

10 bək̠ol-libbî d̠əraštî́k̠ā
ᵓal-tašgḗnî mimmiṣwōt̠eʸ́k̠ā

With my whole heart have I sought Thee;
O let me not err from Thy commandments.

11 bəlibbî ṣāp̄ánti ʾimrāṯéḵā
lǝmáʿan lōʾ ʾeḥĕṭāʾ-lāḵ

Thy word have I laid up in my heart,
that I might not sin against Thee.

12 bārûḵ ʾattāʰ yhwh(ʾăḏōnāy)
lammǝḏḗnî ḥuqqeʸ́ḵā

Blessed art Thou, O LORD;
teach me Thy statutes.

13 biśp̄āṯay sippártî
kōl mišpǝṭê-p̄îḵā

With my lips have I told
all the ordinances of Thy mouth.

14 bǝḏéreḵ ʿēḏwōṯeʸ́ḵā śáśtî
kǝʿal kol-hôn

I have rejoiced in the way of Thy testimonies,
as much as in all riches.

15 bǝp̄iqqūḏeʸ́ḵā ʾāśî́ḥāʰ
wǝʾabbî́ṭāʰ ʾōrḥōṯeʸ́ḵā

I will meditate in Thy precepts,
and have respect unto Thy ways.

16 bǝḥuqqōṯeʸ́ḵā ʾeštaʿăšāʿ
lōʾ ʾeškaḥ dǝḇāréḵā

I will delight myself in Thy statutes;
I will not forget Thy word. {P}

GIMEL. [ג]

17 gǝmōl ʿal-ʿaḇdǝḵā ʾeḥyeʰ
wǝʾešmǝrāʰ ḏǝḇāréḵā

Deal bountifully with Thy servant that I may live,
and I will observe Thy word.

18 gal-ʿênay wǝʾabbî́ṭāʰ
nip̄lāʾôṯ mittôrāṯéḵā

Open Thou mine eyes, that I may behold
wondrous things out of Thy law.

19 gēr ʾānōḵî ḇāʾā́reṣ
ʾal-tastēr mimménnî miṣwōṯeʸ́ḵā

I am a sojourner in the earth;
hide not Thy commandments from me.

20 gārsāʰ nap̄šî lǝṯaʾăḇāʰ
ʾel-mišpāṭeʸ́ḵā ḇǝḵol-ʿēṯ

My soul breaketh for the longing that it hath
unto Thine ordinances at all times.

21 gāʿartā zēḏîm ʾărûrîm
haššōḡîm mimmiṣwōṯeʸ́ḵā

Thou hast rebuked the proud that are cursed,
that do err from Thy commandments.

22 gal mēʿālay ḥerpāʰ wāḇûz
kî ʿēḏōṯeʸ́ḵā nāṣā́rtî

Take away from me reproach and contempt;
for I have kept Thy testimonies.

23 gam yāšḇû śārîm bî niḏbā́rû
ʿaḇdǝḵā yāśîᵃḥ bǝḥuqqeʸ́ḵā

Even though princes sit and talk against me,
thy servant doth meditate in Thy statutes.

24 gam-ʿēḏōṯeʸḵā šaʿăšūʿāy
ʾanšê ʿăṣāṯî

Yea, Thy testimonies are my delight,
they are my counsellors. {P}

DALETH. [ד]

25 dāḇqāʰ leʿāp̄ār nap̄šî
ḥayyḗnî kiḏḇāréḵā

My soul cleaveth unto the dust;
quicken Thou me according to Thy word.

26 dǝrāḵay sippartî wattaʿănḗnî
lammǝḏḗnî ḥuqqeʸ́ḵā

I told of my ways, and Thou didst answer me;
teach me Thy statutes.

27 dereḵ-piqqûḏeʸ́ḵā hăḇînḗnî
wǝʾāśî́ḥāʰ bǝnip̄lǝʾôṯeʸ́ḵā

Make me to understand the way of Thy precepts,
that I may talk of Thy wondrous works.

28 dālp̄āʰ nap̄šî mittûḡāʰ
qayyǝmḗnî kiḏḇāréḵā

My soul melteth away for heaviness;
sustain me according unto Thy word.

29 dęrek-šeqer hāsēr mimménnî
wǝṯôrāṯkā ḥonnḗnî

Remove from me the way of falsehood;
and grant me Thy law graciously.

30 dęrek-ʾĕmûnā^h ḇāḥā́rtî
mišpāṭe^{y}kā šiwwî́ṯî

I have chosen the way of faithfulness;
Thine ordinances have I set [before me].

31 dāḇáqtî ḇǝʿēḏwōṯe^{y}ḵā
yhwh(ʾăḏōnāy) ʾal-tǝḇîšḗnî

I cleave unto Thy testimonies;
O LORD, put me not to shame.

32 dęrek-miṣwōṯe^{y}ḵā ʾārûṣ
kî ṯarḥîḇ libbî

I will run the way of Thy commandments,
for Thou dost enlarge my heart. {P}

HE. [ה]

33 hôrḗnî yhwh(ʾăḏōnāy) dérek ḥuqqe^{y}ḵā
wǝʾeṣṣǝrénnā^h ʿḗqeḇ

Teach me, O LORD, the way of Thy statutes;
and I will keep it at every step.

34 hăḇînēnî wǝʾeṣṣǝrā^h ṯôrāṯéḵā
wǝʾešmǝrénnā^h ḇǝḵol-lēḇ

Give me understanding, that I keep Thy law
and observe it with my whole heart.

35 hadrîḵēnî binṯîḇ miṣwōṯe^{y}ḵā
kî-ḇô ḥāp̄ā́ṣtî

Make me to tread in the path of Thy commandments;
for therein do I delight.

36 haṭ-libbî ʾel-ʿēḏwōṯe^{y}ḵā
wǝʾal ʾel-bā́ṣaʿ

Incline my heart unto Thy testimonies,
and not to covetousness.

37 haʿăḇēr ʿênay mērʾôṯ šā́wʾ
biḏrāḵéḵā ḥayyḗnî

Turn away mine eyes from beholding vanity,
and quicken me in Thy ways.

38 hāqēm lǝʿaḇdǝḵā ʾimrāṯéḵā
ʾăšer lǝyirʾāṯéḵā

Confirm Thy word unto Thy servant,
which pertaineth unto the fear of Thee.

39 haʿăḇēr ḥerpāṯî ʾăšer yāḡṓrtî
kî mišpāṭe^{y}ḵā ṭôḇîm

Turn away my reproach which I dread;
for Thine ordinances are good.

40 hinnē^h tāʾáḇtî lǝp̄iqqūḏe^{y}ḵā
bǝṣiḏqāṯkā ḥayyḗnî

Behold, I have longed after Thy precepts;
quicken me in Thy righteousness. {P}

VAV. [ו]

41 wîḇōʾū́nî ḥăsāḏéḵā yhwh(ʾăḏōnāy)
tǝšû́ʿāṯkā kǝʾimrāṯéḵā

Let Thy mercies also come unto me, O LORD,
even Thy salvation, according to Thy word;

42 wǝʾęʿĕne^h ḥōrp̄î ḏāḇār
kî-ḇāṭaḥtî biḏḇāréḵā

That I may have an answer for him that taunteth me;
for I trust in Thy word.

43 wǝʾal-taṣṣēl mippî ḏǝḇar-ʾĕmeṯ ʿaḏ-mǝʾōḏ
kî lǝmišpāṭéḵā yiḥā́ltî

And take not the word of truth utterly out of my mouth;
for I hope in Thine ordinances;

44 wǝʾešmǝrā^h ṯôrāṯkā ṯāmîḏ
lǝʿôlām wāʿeḏ

So shall I observe Thy law continually
for ever and ever;

45 wǝʾeṯhallǝḵā^h ḇārǝḥāḇā^h
kî p̄iqqūḏe^{y}ḵā ḏārā́štî

And I will walk at ease,
for I have sought Thy precepts;

46 waʾăḏabbǝrā^h ḇǝʿēḏōṯe^{y}ḵā néḡeḏ mǝlāḵîm
wǝlōʾ ʾēḇôš

I will also speak of Thy testimonies before kings,
and will not be ashamed.

47 wəʾeštaʿăšaʿ bəmiṣwōṯeʸḵā
ʾăšer ʾāhā́ḇtî

And I will delight myself in Thy commandments,
which I have loved.

48 wəʾeśśāʾ-ḵappay
ʾel-miṣwōṯeʸḵā
ʾăšer ʾāhā́ḇtî
wəʾāśî́ḥāʰ ḇəḥuqqeʸ́ḵā

I will lift up my hands also
unto Thy commandments,
which I have loved;
and I will meditate in Thy statutes. {P}

ZAIN. [ז]

49 zəḵōr-dāḇār ləʿaḇdéḵā
ʿal ʾăšer yiḥaltā́nî

Remember the word unto Thy servant,
because Thou hast made me to hope.

50 zōʾṯ neḥāmāṯî ḇəʿonyî
kî ʾimrāṯḵā ḥiyyā́ṯnî

This is my comfort in my affliction,
that Thy word hath quickened me.

51 zēḏîm hĕlîṣū́nî ʿaḏ-məʾōḏ
mittôrāṯḵā lōʾ nāṭî́ṯî

The proud have had me greatly in derision;
yet have I not turned aside from Thy law.

52 zāḵártî mišpāṭeʸ́ḵā mēʿôlām
yhwh(ʾăḏōnāy) wāʾeṯneḥām

I have remembered Thine ordinances which are of old,
O LORD, and have comforted myself.

53 zalʿāpāʰ ʾăḥāzaṯnî mēršāʿîm
ʿōzḇê tôrāṯéḵā

Burning indignation hath taken hold upon me, because of the wicked
that forsake Thy law.

54 zəmīrôṯ hāyû-lî ḥuqqeʸ́ḵā
bəḇêṯ məḡûrāy

Thy statutes have been my songs
in the house of my pilgrimage.

55 zāḵártî ḇalláylāʰ šimḵā yhwh(ʾăḏōnāy)
wāʾešmərāʰ tôrāṯéḵā

I have remembered Thy name, O LORD, in the night,
and have observed Thy law.

56 zōʾṯ hāyṯāʰ-llî
kî p̄iqqūḏeʸ́ḵā nāṣā́rtî

This I have had,
that I have kept Thy precepts. {P}

HETH. [ח]

57 ḥelqî yhwh(ʾăḏōnāy) ʾāmártî
lišmōr dəḇāreʸ́ḵā

My portion is the LORD, I have said [that]
I would observe Thy words.

58 ḥillî́ṯî p̄āneʸ́ḵā ḇəḵol-lēḇ
ḥonnḗnî kəʾimrāṯéḵā

I have entreated Thy favour with my whole heart;
be gracious unto me according to Thy word.

59 ḥiššáḇtî ḏərāḵāy
wāʾāšî́ḇāʰ raḡlay ʾel-ʿēḏōṯeʸ́ḵā

I considered my ways,
and turned my feet unto Thy testimonies.

60 ḥaštî wəlōʾ hiṯmahmā́htî
lišmōr miṣwōṯeʸ́ḵā

I made haste, and delayed not,
to observe Thy commandments.

61 ḥeḇlê rəšāʿîm ʿiwwəḏū́nî
tôrāṯḵā lōʾ šāḵā́ḥtî

The bands of the wicked have enclosed me;
but I have not forgotten Thy law.

62 ḥăṣôṯ-láylāʰ ʾāqûm ləhôḏôṯ lāḵ
ʿal mišpəṭê ṣiḏqéḵā

At midnight I will rise to give thanks unto Thee
because of Thy righteous ordinances.

63 ḥāḇēr ʾānî ləḵol-ʾăšer yərēʾū́ḵā
ûləšōmrê piqqûḏeʸ́ḵā

I am a companion of all them that fear Thee,
and of them that observe Thy precepts.

64 ḥasdəḵā yhwh(ʾăḏōnāy) mālʾāʰ hāʾāreṣ
ḥuqqeʸ́ḵā lamməḏḗnî

The earth, O LORD, is full of Thy mercy;
teach me Thy statutes. {P}

TETH. [ט]

65 ṭôḇ ʿāśî́ṯā ʿịm-ʿaḇdəḵā
yhwh(ʾăḏōnāy) kiḏḇāréḵā

Thou hast dealt well with Thy servant,
O LORD, according unto Thy word.

66 ṭûḇ ṭáʿam wāḏáʿaṯ lammәḏḗnî
kî ḇəmiṣwōṯeʸḵā heʾĕmā́ntî

Teach me good discernment and knowledge;
for I have believed in Thy commandments.

67 ṭérem ʾeʿĕneʰ ʾănî šōḡēḡ
wəʿattāʰ ʾimrāṯḵā šāmā́rtî

Before I was afflicted, I did err;
but now I observe Thy word.

68 ṭôḇ-ʾattāʰ ûmēṭîḇ
lammәḏḗnî ḥuqqeʸḵā

Thou art good, and doest good;
teach me Thy statutes.

69 ṭāp̄lû ʿālay šéqer zēḏîm
ʾănî bəḵol-lēḇ ʾĕṣṣōr piqqûḏeʸḵā

The proud have forged a lie against me;
but I with my whole heart will keep Thy precepts.

70 ṭāp̄aš kaḥḗleḇ libbām
ʾănî tôrāṯḵā šịʿăšā́ʿtî

Their heart is gross like fat;
but I delight in Thy law.

71 ṭộḇ-lî ḵị̂-ʿunnḗṯî
ləmáʿan ʾelmaḏ ḥuqqeʸḵā

It is good for me that I have been afflicted,
in order that I might learn Thy statutes.

72 ṭộḇ-lî ṯộraṯ-pî́ḵā
mēʾalp̄ê zāhāḇ wāḵā́sep̄

The law of Thy mouth is better unto me
than thousands of gold and silver. {P}

YOD. [י]

73 yāḏeʸḵā ʿāśûnî wạyəḵônənû́nî
hăḇînḗnî wəʾelməḏāʰ miṣwōṯeʸḵā

Thy hands have made me and fashioned me;
give me understanding, that I may learn Thy commandments.

74 yərēʾeʸḵā yirʾû́nî wəyiśmā́ḥû
kî liḏḇārḵā yiḥā́ltî

They that fear Thee shall see me and be glad,
because I have hope in Thy word.

75 yāḏáʿtî yhwh(ʾăḏōnāy) kî-ṣéḏeq mišpāṭeʸḵā
weʾĕmûnāʰ ʿinnîṯā́nî

I know, O LORD, that Thy judgments are righteous,
and that in faithfulness Thou hast afflicted me.

76 yəhî-nāʾ ḥasdəḵā lənaḥămḗnî
kəʾimrāṯḵā ləʿaḇdéḵā

Let, I pray Thee, Thy lovingkindness be ready to comfort me,
according to Thy promise unto Thy servant.

77 yəḇōʾû́nî raḥămeʸḵā wəʾẹḥyeʰ
kî-ṯộrāṯḵā šạʿăšūʿāy

Let Thy tender mercies come unto me, that I may live;
for Thy law is my delight.

78 yēḇṓšû zēḏîm kî-šéqer ʿiwwəṯû́nî
ʾănî ʾāśîᵃḥ bəp̄iqqûḏeʸḵā

Let the proud be put to shame, for they have distorted my cause with falsehood;
but I will meditate in Thy precepts.

79 yāšû́ḇû lî yərēʾeʸḵā
(K:wəyāḏʿû) [Q:wəyōḏʿê] ʿēḏōṯeʸḵā

Let those that fear Thee return unto me,
and they that know Thy testimonies.

80 yəhị̂-libbî ṯāmîm bəḥuqqeʸḵā
ləmáʿan lōʾ ʾēḇôš

Let my heart be undivided in Thy statutes,
in order that I may not be put to shame. {P}

KAPH. [כ]

81 kālṯāʰ liṯšûʿāṯḵā nap̄šî
liḏḇārḵā yiḥā́ltî

My soul pineth for Thy salvation;
in Thy word do I hope.

82 kālû ʿênay ləʾimrāṯéḵā
lēʾmōr māṯay tẹnaḥămḗnî

Mine eyes fail for Thy word, saying:
'When wilt Thou comfort me?'

83 kị̂-hāyîṯî kənōᵓḏ bəqîṭôr
huqqe$^{\acute{y}}$ḵā lōᵓ šāḵā́ḥtî

For I am become like a wine-skin in the smoke;
yet do I not forget Thy statutes.

84 kammā^{h} yəmệ-ᶜaḇdéḵā
māṯay taᶜăśe^{h} ḇərōḏp̄ay mišpāṭ

How many are the days of Thy servant?
When wilt Thou execute judgment on them that persecute me?

85 kạ̄rû-lî zēḏîm šîḥôṯ
ᵓăšer lōᵓ ḵəṯôrāṯéḵā

The proud have digged pits for me,
which is not according to Thy law.

86 kol-miṣwōṯe$^{\acute{y}}$ḵā ᵓĕmûnā^{h}
šéqer rəḏāp̄ū́nî ᶜozrḗnî

All Thy commandments are faithful;
they persecute me for nought; help Thou me.

87 kimᶜaṭ killū́nî ḇāᵓā́reṣ
waᵓănî lōᵓ-ᶜāzáḇtî p̄iqquwḏe$^{\acute{y}}$ḵā

They had almost consumed me upon earth;
but as for me, I forsook not Thy precepts.

88 kəḥasdəḵā ḥayyḗnî
wəᵓešmərā^{h} ᶜēḏûṯ pî́ḵā

Quicken me after Thy lovingkindness,
and I will observe the testimony of Thy mouth. {P}

LAMED. [ל]

89 ləᶜôlām yhwh(ᵓāḏōnāy)
dəḇārḵā niṣṣāḇ baššāmā́yim

For ever, O LORD,
Thy word standeth fast in heaven.

90 ləḏōr wāḏōr ᵓĕmûṇāṯéḵā
kônántā ᵓéreṣ wạttaᶜămōḏ

Thy faithfulness is unto all generations;
Thou hast established the earth, and it standeth.

91 lạmišpāṭe^{y}ḵā ᶜāmḏû hayyôm
kî hakkōl ᶜăḇāḏe$^{\acute{y}}$ḵā

They stand this day according to Thine ordinances;
for all things are Thy servants.

92 lûlê ṯôrāṯḵā šaᶜăšūᶜāy
ᵓāz ᵓāḇáḏtî ḇəᶜonyî

Unless Thy law had been my delight,
I should then have perished in mine affliction.

93 ləᶜôlām lōᵓ-ᵓeškaḥ piqqûḏe^{y}ḵā
kî ḇām ḥiyyîṯā́nî

I will never forget Thy precepts;
for with them Thou hast quickened me.

94 lạḵā-ᵓănî hôšîᶜḗnî
kî p̄iqqûḏe$^{\acute{y}}$ḵā ḏārā́štî

I am Thine, save me;
for I have sought Thy precepts.

95 lî qiwwû rəšāᶜîm ləᵓabbəḏḗnî
ᶜēḏōṯe$^{\acute{y}}$ḵā ᵓeṯbônān

The wicked have waited for me to destroy me;
but I will consider Thy testimonies.

96 lạḵāl tiḵlā^{h} rāᵓî́ṯî qēṣ
rəḥāḇā^{h} miṣwāṯḵā məᵓōḏ

I have seen an end to every purpose;
but Thy commandment is exceeding broad. {P}

MEM. [מ]

97 mā^{h}-ᵓāháḇtî ṯôrāṯéḵā
kol-hayyôm hîᵓ śîḥāṯî

O how love I Thy law!
It is my meditation all the day.

98 mēᵓō̃yḇay təḥakkəmḗnî miṣwōṯéḵā
kî ləᶜôlām hîᵓ-lî

Thy commandments make me wiser than mine enemies:
for they are ever with me.

99 mikkol-məlamməḏay hiśkáltî
kî ᶜēḏwōṯe$^{\acute{y}}$ḵā śî́ḥā^{h} lî

I have more understanding than all my teachers;
for Thy testimonies are my meditation.

100 mizzəqēnîm ᵓeṯbônān
kî p̄iqqûḏe$^{\acute{y}}$ḵā nāṣā́rtî

I understand more than mine elders,
because I have keep Thy precepts.

101 mikkol-ʾṓraḥ rāʿ kālíʾṯî raḡlāy
ləmáʿan ʾešmōr dəḇārékā

I have refrained my feet from every evil way,
in order that I might observe Thy word.

102 mimmišpāṭeʸ́ḵā lōʾ-sā́rtî
kî-ʾattāʰ hôrēṯā́nî

I have not turned aside from Thine ordinances;
for Thou hast instructed me.

103 maʰ-nnimləṣû ləḥikkî ʾimrāṯéḵā
middəḇaš ləp̄î

How sweet are Thy words unto my palate!
yea, sweeter than honey to my mouth!

104 mippiqqûḏeʸ́ḵā ʾeṯbônān
ʿal-kēn śānḗʾṯî kol-ʾṓraḥ šā́qer

From Thy precepts I get understanding;
therefore I hate every false way. {P}

NUN. [נ]

105 nēr-ləraḡlî ḏəḇārékā
wəʾôr linṯîḇāṯî

Thy word is a lamp unto my feet,
and a light unto my path.

106 nišbáʿtî wāʾăqayyḗmāʰ
lišmōr mišpəṭê ṣiḏqéḵā

I have sworn, and have confirmed it,
to observe Thy righteous ordinances.

107 naʿănḗṯî ʿaḏ-məʾōḏ
yhwh(ʾăḏōnāy) ḥayyḗnî kiḏḇārékā

I am afflicted very much; quicken me,
O LORD, according unto Thy word.

108 niḏḇôṯ pî rəṣēʰ-nāʾ yhwh(ʾăḏōnāy)
ûmišpāṭeʸ́ḵā lammədḗnî

Accept, I beseech Thee, the freewill-offerings of my mouth, O LORD,
and teach me Thine ordinances.

109 nap̄šî ḇəḵappî ṯāmîḏ
wəṯôrāṯḵā lōʾ šāḵā́ḥtî

My soul is continually in my hand;
yet have I not forgotten Thy law.

110 nāṯnû rəšāʿîm paḥ lî
ûmippiqqûḏeʸ́ḵā lōʾ ṯāʿî́ṯî

The wicked have laid a snare for me;
yet went I not astray from Thy precepts.

111 nāḥáltî ʿēḏwōṯeʸ́ḵā ləʿôlām
kî-śəśôn libbî hḗmmāʰ

Thy testimonies have I taken as a heritage for ever;
for they are the rejoicing of my heart.

112 nāṭī́ṯî libbî laʿăśôṯ ḥuqqeʸ́ḵā
ləʿôlām ʿḗqeḇ

I have inclined my heart to perform Thy statutes,
for ever, at every step. {P}

SAMECH. [ס]

113 sēʿăp̄îm śānḗʾṯî
wəṯôrāṯḵā ʾāhā́ḇtî

I hate them that are of a double mind;
but Thy law do I love.

114 siṯrî ûmāḡinnî ʾā́ttāʰ
liḏḇārḵā yiḥā́ltî

Thou art my covert and my shield;
in Thy word do I hope.

115 sûrû-mimménnî mərēʿîm
wəʾeṣṣərāʰ miṣwōṯ ʾĕlōhāy

Depart from me, ye evildoers;
that I may keep the commandments of my God.

116 somḵḗnî ḵəʾimrāṯḵā wəʾeḥyeʰ
wəʾal-təḇîšḗnî miśśiḇrî

Uphold me according unto Thy word, that I may live;
and put me not to shame in my hope.

117 səʿāḏḗnî wəʾiwwāšḗʿāʰ
wəʾešʿāʰ ḇəḥuqqeʸ́ḵā ṯāmîḏ

Support Thou me, and I shall be saved;
and I will occupy myself with Thy statutes continually.

118 sālîṯā kol-šôḡîm mēḥuqqeʸ́ḵā
kî-šéqer tarmîṯām

Thou hast made light of all them that err from Thy statutes;
for their deceit is vain.

119 sīḡîm hišbáttā ḵol-rišʿê-ʾā́reṣ
    lāḵēn ʾāháḇtî ʿēḏōṯeʸ́ḵā

Thou puttest away all the wicked of the earth like dross;
    therefore I love Thy testimonies.

120 sāmar mippaḥdəḵā ḇəśārî
    ûmimmišpāṭeʸ́ḵā yārḗʾṯî

My flesh shuddereth for fear of Thee;
    and I am afraid of Thy judgments. {P}

ʿAIN. [ע]

121 ʿāśîṯî mišpāṭ wāṣéḏeq
    bal-tannîḥḗnî ləʿōšqāy

I have done justice and righteousness;
    leave me not to mine oppressors.

122 ʿărōḇ ʿaḇdəḵā ləṭôḇ
    ʾal-yaʿašqū́nî zēḏîm

Be surety for Thy servant for good;
    let not the proud oppress me.

123 ʿênay kālû lîšûʿāṯéḵā
    ûləʾimraṯ ṣiḏqéḵā

Mine eyes fail for Thy salvation,
    and for Thy righteous word.

124 ʿăśēʰ ʿim-ʿaḇdəḵā ḵəḥasdéḵā
    wəḥuqqeʸ́ḵā lamməḏḗnî

Deal with Thy servant according unto Thy mercy,
    and teach me Thy statutes.

125 ʿaḇdəḵā-ʾā́nî hăḇînḗnî
    wəʾēḏʿāʰ ʿēḏōṯeʸ́ḵā

I am Thy servant, give me understanding,
    that I may know Thy testimonies.

126 ʿēṯ laʿăśôṯ lyhwh(laʾḏōnāy)
    hēp̄ḗrû tôrāṯéḵā

It is time for the LORD to work;
    they have made void Thy law.

127 ʿal-kēn ʾāháḇtî miṣwōṯeʸ́ḵā
    mizzāhāḇ ûmippāz

Therefore I love Thy commandments
    above gold, yea, above fine gold.

128 ʿal-kēn kol-piqqū́ḏê ḵōl yiššā́rtî
    kol-ʾṓraḥ šéqer śānḗʾṯî

Therefore I esteem all … precepts concerning all things to be right;
    every false way I hate. {P}

PE. [פ]

129 pəlāʾôṯ ʿēḏwōṯeʸ́ḵā
    ʿal-kēn nəṣārā́ṯam nap̄šî

Thy testimonies are wonderful;
    therefore doth my soul keep them.

130 pḗṯaḥ dəḇāreʸ́ḵā yāʾîr
    mēḇîn pəṯāyîm

The opening of Thy words giveth light;
    it giveth understanding unto the simple.

131 pî-p̄āʿartî wāʾešʾā́p̄āʰ
    kî ləmiṣwōṯeʸ́ḵā yāʾā́ḇtî

I opened wide my mouth, and panted;
    for I longed for Thy commandments.

132 pənēʰ-ʾēlay wəḥonnḗnî
    kəmišpāṭ ləʾōhăḇê šəméḵā

Turn Thee towards me, and be gracious unto me,
    as is Thy wont to do unto those that love Thy name.

133 pəʿāmay hāḵēn bəʾimrāṯéḵā
    wəʾal-tašleṭ-bî ḵol-ʾā́wen

Order my footsteps by Thy word;
    and let not any iniquity have dominion over me.

134 pəḏēnî mēʿṓšeq ʾāḏām
    wəʾešmərāʰ piqqûḏeʸ́ḵā

Redeem me from the oppression of man,
    and I will observe Thy precepts.

135 pāneʸḵā hāʾēr bəʿaḇdéḵā
    wəlamməḏḗnî ʾeṯ-ḥuqqeʸ́ḵā

Make Thy face to shine upon Thy servant;
    and teach me Thy statutes.

136 palḡê-mayīm yārḏû ʿênāy
    ʿal lōʾ-šāmrû ṯôrāṯéḵā

Mine eyes run down with rivers of water,
    because they observe not Thy law. {P}

TZADE. [צ]

137 ṣaddîq ʾattā^{h} yhwh(ʾăḏōnāy)
wəyāšār mišpāṭe^{ý}ḵā

Righteous art Thou, O LORD,
and upright are Thy judgments.

138 ṣiwwîṯā ṣéḏeq ʿēḏōṯe^{ý}ḵā
wẹʾĕmûnā^{h} məʾōḏ

Thou hast commanded Thy testimonies in righteousness
and exceeding faithfulness.

139 ṣimmətáṯnî qinʾāṯî
kị-šāḵḥû ḏəḇāre^{ý}ḵā ṣārāy

My zeal hath undone me,
because mine adversaries have forgotten Thy words.

140 ṣərûpā^{h} ʾimrāṯḵā məʾōḏ
wẹʿaḇdəḵā ʾăhēḇāh

Thy word is tried to the uttermost,
and Thy servant loveth it.

141 ṣāʿîr ʾānōḵî wəniḇze^{h}
piqqūḏe^{ý}ḵā lōʾ šāḵā́ḥtî

I am small and despised;
yet have I not forgotten Thy precepts.

142 ṣiḏqāṯḵā ṣéḏeq ləʿôlām
wẹṯôrāṯḵā ʾĕmeṯ

Thy righteousness is an everlasting righteousness,
and Thy law is truth.

143 ṣar-ûmāṣôq məṣāʾū́nî
miṣwōṯe^{ý}ḵā šaʿăšūʿāy

Trouble and anguish have overtaken me;
yet Thy commandments are my delight.

144 ṣéḏeq ʿēḏwōṯe^{ý}ḵā ləʿôlām
hăḇînḗnî wəʾeḥye^{h}

Thy testimonies are righteous for ever;
give me understanding, and I shall live. {P}

QOPH. [ק]

145 qārā́ʾṯî ḇəḵol-lēḇ ʿănḗnî yhwh(ʾăḏōnāy)
ḥuqqe^{ý}ḵā ʾeṣṣṓrā^{h}

I have called with my whole heart; answer me, O LORD;
I will keep Thy statutes.

146 qərāʾṯī́ḵā hôšîʿḗnî
wəʾešmərā^{h} ʿēḏōṯe^{ý}ḵā

I have called Thee, save me,
and I will observe Thy testimonies.

147 qiddámtî ḇannešep̄ wāʾăšawwḗʿā^{h}
(^{K}lidḇāre^{y}ḵā) [^{Q}lidḇārḵā] yiḥā́ltî

I rose early at dawn, and cried;
I hoped in Thy word.

148 qiddəmû ʿênay ʾašmūrôṯ
lāśîªḥ bəʾimrāṯéḵā

Mine eyes forestalled the night-watches,
that I might meditate in Thy word.

149 qôlî šimʿā^{h} ḵəḥasdéḵā
yhwh(ʾăḏōnāy) kẹmišpāṭéḵā ḥayyḗnî

Hear my voice according unto Thy lovingkindness;
quicken me, O LORD, as Thou art wont.

150 qārḇû rōḏp̄ê zimmā^{h}
mittôrāṯḵā rāḥā́qû

They draw nigh that follow after wickedness;
they are far from Thy law.

151 qārôḇ ʾattā^{h} yhwh(ʾăḏōnāy)
wẹḵol-miṣwōṯe^{ý}ḵā ʾĕmeṯ

Thou art nigh, O LORD;
and all Thy commandments are truth.

152 qéḏem yāḏaʿtî mēʿēḏōṯe^{ý}ḵā
kî ləʿôlām yəsaḏtām

Of old have I known from Thy testimonies
that Thou hast founded them for ever. {P}

RESH. [ר]

153 rəʾē^{h}-ʿonyî wəḥalləṣḗnî
kî-ṯọrāṯḵā lōʾ šāḵā́ḥtî

O see mine affliction, and rescue me;
for I do not forget Thy law.

154 rîḇā^{h} rîḇî ûḡəʾālḗnî
ləʾimrāṯḵā ḥayyḗnî

Plead Thou my cause, and redeem me;
quicken me according to Thy word.

155 rāḥôq mēršāʿîm yəšûʿāʰ
kị-ḥuqqeʸkā lōʾ ḏārā́šû

Salvation is far from the wicked;
for they seek not Thy statutes.

156 raḥămeʸ́ḵā rabbîm yhwh(ʾăḏōnāy)
kə̣mišpāṭeʸ́ḵā ḥayyḗnî

Great are Thy compassions, O LORD;
quicken me as Thou art wont.

157 rabbîm rōḏp̄ay wəṣāray
mēʿēḏwōṯeʸ́ḵā lōʾ nāṭî́ṯî

Many are my persecutors and mine adversaries;
yet have I not turned aside from Thy testimonies.

158 rāʾî́ṯî ḇōḡḏîm wā̦ʾeṯqôṭā́ṭāʰ
ʾăšer ʾimrāṯḵā lōʾ šāmā́rû

I beheld them that were faithless, and strove with them;
because they observed not Thy word.

159 rəʾēʰ kî-p̄iqqûḏeʸ́ḵā ʾāhā́ḇtî
yhwh(ʾăḏōnāy) kə̣ḥasdəḵā ḥayyḗnî

O see how I love Thy precepts;
quicken me, O LORD, according to Thy lovingkindness.

160 rōʾš-dəḇārḵā ʾĕmeṯ
ûləʿôlām kol-mišpaṭ ṣiḏqéḵā

The beginning of Thy word is truth;
and all Thy righteous ordinance endureth for ever. {P}

SHIN. [ש]

161 śārîm rəḏāp̄ū́nî ḥinnām
(ᴷ:ûmiddəḇāreʸḵā) [Q:ûmiddəḇārḵā] pāḥaḏ libbî

Princes have persecuted me without a cause;
but my heart standeth in awe of Thy words.

162 śāś ʾānōḵị ʿal-ʾimrāṯéḵā
kəmôṣēʾ šālāl rāḇ

I rejoice at Thy word,
as one that findeth great spoil.

163 šéqer śānēʾṯî waʾăṯaʿḗḇāʰ
tôrāṯḵā ʾāhā́ḇtî

I hate and abhor falsehood;
Thy law do I love.

164 šéḇaʿ bayyôm hillaltî́ḵā
ʿal mišpəṭê ṣiḏqéḵā

Seven times a day do I praise Thee,
because of Thy righteous ordinances.

165 šālôm rāḇ ləʾōhăḇê ṯôrāṯéḵā
wəʾện-lā́mô miḵšôl

Great peace have they that love Thy law;
and there is no stumbling for them.

166 śibbártî lị̂šûʿāṯḵā yhwh(ʾăḏōnāy)
ụ̂miṣwōṯeʸ́ḵā ʿāśî́ṯî

I have hoped for Thy salvation, O LORD,
and have done Thy commandments.

167 šā̦mrāʰ nap̄šî ʿēḏōṯeʸ́ḵā
wāʾōhăḇēm məʾōḏ

My soul hath observed Thy testimonies;
and I love them exceedingly.

168 šāmártî p̄iqqûḏeʸḵā wəʿēḏōṯeʸḵā
kî ḵol-dərāḵay neḡdéḵā

I have observed Thy precepts and Thy testimonies;
for all my ways are before Thee. {P}

TAU. [ת]

169 tiqraḇ rinnāṯî ləp̄āneʸ́ḵā yhwh(ʾăḏōnāy)
kiḏḇārḵā hăḇînḗnî

Let my cry come near before Thee, O LORD;
give me understanding according to Thy word.

170 tāḇôʾ təḥinnāṯî ləp̄āneʸḵā
kəʾimrāṯḵā haṣṣîlḗnî

Let my supplication come before Thee;
deliver me according to Thy word.

171 tabbáʿnāʰ śəp̄āṯay təhillāʰ
kî ṯəlamməḏḗnî ḥuqqeʸ́ḵā

Let my lips utter praise:
because Thou teachest me Thy statutes.

172 táʿan ləšônî ʾimrāṯéḵā
kî ḵol-miṣwōṯeʸ́ḵā ṣṣeḏeq

Let my tongue sing of Thy word;
for all Thy commandments are righteousness.

173 təhî̩-yāḏḵā ləʿozrḗnî kî p̄iqqûḏeʸ́ḵā ḇāḥā́rtî	Let Thy hand be ready to help me; for I have chosen Thy precepts.
174 tāʾáḇtî lî̩šûʿāṯḵā yhwh(ʾăḏōnāy) wəṯô̩rāṯḵā šaʿăšūʿāy	I have longed for Thy salvation, O LORD; and Thy law is my delight.
175 tə̩ḥî-nap̄šî û̩ṯəhaֽ̩ləlékkā û̩mišpāṭéḵā yaʿăzrū́nî	Let my soul live, and it shall praise Thee; and let Thine ordinances help me.
176 tāʿî́ṯî kəśeʰ ʾōḇēḏ baqqēš ʿaḇdéḵā kî miṣwōṯeʸ́ḵā lōʾ šāḵā́ḥtî	I have gone astray like a lost sheep; seek Thy servant; {N} for I have not forgotten Thy commandments. {P}

ADDITIONAL RESOURCES

In preparing to write and teach *Blessings Beyond the Page: A Study of Psalm 119,* I found four studies immensely helpful. Because of how much they shaped and enriched my view of the psalms, I would like to acknowledge those studies here.

Kidner, Derek. *Psalms 73–150, Tyndale Old Testament Commentaries.* Edited by D. J. Wiseman. Westmont, Illinois: Inter Varsity Press, 1975.

Radmacher, Earl. *Nelson's Compact Series: Compact Bible Commentary.* Edited by Ron Allen and Wayne House. Nashville, TN: Thomas Nelson, 2004.

Wiersbe, Warren W. *Prayer, Praise & Promises: A Daily Walk Through the Psalms.* Lincoln, NE: Back to the Bible, 2013.

Wiersbe, Warren W. *With the Word: The Chapter-by-Chapter Bible Handbook.* Nashville, TN: Thomas Nelson, 1991

www.ingramcontent.com/pod-product-compliance
Lightning Source LLC
Chambersburg PA
CBHW072013090426
42740CB00011B/2180

9781632967015